A Clinical Reference

Carole T. Ferrand

An International Publisher

8700 Shoal Creek Boulevard
Austin, Texas 78757-6897
800/897-3202   Fax 800/397-7633
www.proedinc.com

© 2008 by PRO-ED, Inc.
8700 Shoal Creek Boulevard
Austin, Texas 78757-6897
800/897-3202   Fax 800/397-7633
www.proedinc.com

Library of Congress Cataloging-in-Publication Data

Ferrand, Carole T.
   Voice disorders : a clinical reference / Carole T. Ferrand.
       p. ; cm.
   Includes bibliographical references.
   ISBN-13: 978-1-4164-0252-7
   ISBN-10: 1-4164-0257-8
   1. Voice disorders—Diagnosis. I. Title.
   [DNLM: 1. Voice Disorders—diagnosis. 2. Laryngeal Diseases.
3. Voice Disorders—therapy. WV 500 F372v 2008]
   RF510.F48 2008
   616.85'56075—dc22

                                                            2007033799

Art Director: Jason Crosier
Designer: Nancy McKinney-Point
This book is designed in Sabon and Helvetica.

Printed in the United States of America

1   2   3   4   5   6   7   8   9   10   11   10   09   08   07

Contents

Introduction

This book on disorders that affect the voice in various ways is meant for practicing professionals who would appreciate an up-to-date yet easy-to-read reference. Based on my 15 years of experience teaching a graduate-level voice disorders course, *Voice Disorders: A Clinical Reference* is designed to present current knowledge about diagnostic issues and the major categories of voice disorders in a way that is readily accessible to readers. Because the book is designed for practicing professionals, it assumes that readers have knowledge of the anatomical and physiological bases of voice production. However, for quick reference, Appendix A provides a brief overview of laryngeal structures including bone, cartilages, joints, extrinsic membranes, valves, and extrinsic and intrinsic laryngeal muscles. Readers who would appreciate a more detailed review of laryngeal anatomy and physiology will find many excellent texts that present in-depth material, such as that by Colton, Casper, and Leonard (2006). Appendix B provides definitions of currently used terms to facilitate a standardized context and reference for further discussion. Appendix C provides a list of informative Websites.

Chapter 1 begins with a discussion of evaluation strategies and issues, including the importance of administering a quality of life assessment tool to the client, in addition to taking perceptual, acoustic, and physiological measures. The importance of obtaining a thorough case history is emphasized. Different formats for auditory–perceptual ratings are provided, including equal-appearing interval scales, semantic differential scales, and visual analog scales. Commonly used acoustic measures are described, including fundamental frequency, frequency variability, maximum phonational frequency range, and intensity.

Chapter 2 provides a discussion of congenital and acquired structural disorders in children and adults, including disorders such as vocal fold nodules and polyps, contact ulcers, papilloma, subglottic stenosis, laryngeal web, and laryngomalacia. Chapter 3 focuses on disorders resulting from inflammatory conditions of the larynx, such as acute and chronic laryngitis, and laryngopharyngeal reflux; disorders resulting from immune deficiencies and compromised immune systems; paradoxical vocal fold motion; and disorders related to chronic cough. In Chapter 4 the discussion turns to nonorganic disorders that affect the voice, including conversion disorders, gender identity disorders (transsexual and transgender voice), selective mutism, muscle tension dysphonias, and puberphonia. Chapter 5 provides information about neurogenic disorders, classified in terms of flaccid dysphonia, spastic dysphonia, ataxic dysphonia, hypokinetic dysphonia, hyperkinetic dysphonia, and mixed dysphonias. Chapter 6 focuses on malignant laryngeal lesions and laryngectomy, with discussion of medical treatments for removal of the cancer, including radiation therapy, chemotherapy, and different surgical conservation procedures. Total laryngectomy is discussed in terms of problems related to the surgery, communication deficits, and methods of voice restoration.

Chapter 7 concludes the book with discussion of clinical management issues and strategies, categorized in terms of phonosurgical techniques and behavioral voice techniques. Specific procedures are discussed, and behavioral treatment techniques for particular disorders are presented.

Chapter 1
Evaluation of Voice Disorders

Evaluating a voice disorder is a complex task, requiring the clinician to form judgments not only about the voice itself but also about many other factors in the individual's life that can have an impact on vocal production. Thus, the way that the client functions in the emotional, vocational, and social domains is extremely important to take into account, as is the person's physical and mental health status.

An individual with a voice problem is typically seen by an otolaryngologist and a speech–language pathologist. The otolaryngologist assesses the larynx using various methods, including videostroboscopy and indirect or direct laryngoscopy, to detect any structural pathology or functional problems; diagnoses the problem; and decides whether to treat the problem using surgical, pharmacological, and/or behavioral methods. The speech–language pathologist uses auditory–perceptual as well as acoustic and/or aerodynamic means to evaluate the quality, pitch, and loudness characteristics of the voice. The speech–language pathologist investigates the individual's vocal usage in different situations, as well as the person's vocal habits and vocal technique. The clinician usually takes an extensive case history of the patient. The case history seeks medical information regarding coexisting disorders, medications the individual is taking, previous conditions, and onset and course of the disorder. Information regarding the person's emotional status helps to determine whether the client is currently undergoing or has undergone conflict, stress, or anxiety that may contribute to the voice problem. The speech–language pathologist also designs and implements a therapeutic regimen, keeps data regarding vocal function, and documents any changes in the patient's voice. Depending on the individual's vocal problems and needs, other professionals may also be involved in the evaluation process. For example, the client may be referred to a neurologist, pulmonologist, endocrinologist, gastroenterologist, counselor, or social worker.

The voice evaluation is typically divided into several components, as listed in Table 1.1. These include the client interview and case history, as well as perceptual and instrumental assessment of voice. The assessment may also include an oral-motor examination and hearing screening. Once this information has been collected, the speech–language pathologist can interpret the test results and formulate a diagnosis and recommendations (A. F. Johnson, 1994).

Case History

The first step in the evaluation process is usually the case history. The speech–language pathologist gathers information from the client and/or other people in the individual's life about the history and current features of the problem. The case history includes a medical history, social history, and vocational/professional history.

The medical history is important for determining whether and to what extent medically related factors may have

TABLE 1.1 COMPONENTS OF VOICE EVALUATION

Case history	Perceptual measures	Instrumental measures
Demographic	Severity	Laryngoscopy
Medical	Pitch	Endoscopy
Social	Loudness	Videostroboscopy
Vocational	Quality	Acoustic
Professional	Resonance	Aerodynamic

contributed to the development of the voice disorder (Colton, Casper, & Leonard, 2006; Stemple, Glaze, & Klaben, 2000). The client is asked about past surgeries, particularly laryngeal, head and neck, chest, or heart surgeries. If the client has been hospitalized, it is important to learn whether he or she was intubated, and for how long. Questions are asked about the existence of chronic disorders, such as arthritis, and whether the individual uses over-the-counter or prescribed medications. If the client is a female in her 40s or 50s, it is important to find out about the use of hormone replacement therapies. It is also important to probe smoking, drinking, and drug usage habits. Questions should also be asked to determine the existence of any neurological problems, respiratory problems, gastrointestinal tract problems, allergy-related problems, psychiatric problems, congenital anomalies, or hearing loss, as any of these conditions can affect the voice.

When asking about the client's social and professional/vocational life, the speech–language pathologist should focus on probing the amount and type of voice the client uses in different situations and on determining whether the individual is subjected to stress, anxiety, and tension that may contribute to the voice problem. Important topics include the client's home life, family relationships, social network, hobbies, and work- or school-related issues; tobacco, caffeine and alcohol usage; eating habits; and family health history. Many excellent evaluation protocols provide a structured format for obtaining this information (e.g., Boone, McFarlane, & Von Berg, 2005; Koschkee & Rammage, 1997; Mathieson, 2001; Stemple et al., 2000). Most of these protocols seek information about some or all of the following:

- Demographic information
- Nature of the problem
- Duration of the problem
- Tobacco, alcohol, and caffeine consumption
- Daily water intake

- Current and past medications taken
- Surgical history
- Previous conditions and treatment (e.g., neurological, respiratory)
- Formal voice training
- Allergies
- Current and past vocal changes
- Impact of the problem on the client's life

While taking the case history, the clinician has an excellent opportunity to informally evaluate the client's voice in terms of auditory–perceptual characteristics, such as quality (hoarseness, breathiness, strain, tension, weakness, aphonia, voice arrests); pitch level (too low, too high, monopitch, pitch breaks, diplophonia, tremor); loudness level (too soft, too loud, monoloud, uncontrollable bursts of loudness); presence of stridor on inhalation or exhalation, hyper- or hyponasality, hard glottal attacks, and excessive coughing or throat clearing; any observable tension around the client's laryngeal area; and the client's overall posture. Also important is to judge the individual's vocal endurance or fatigue and to note if the voice deteriorates or improves with use during the interview.

As part of the case history, outcome measurement tools such as the Voice Handicap Index (VHI), developed by Jacobson et al. in 1997, are useful in assessing the impact of the voice disorder on the client's life and can also be used to evaluate the outcome of voice therapy. The VHI is a 30-item questionnaire, with questions divided into functional, physical, and emotional categories (see Table 1.2). Each statement is rated on a 5-point scale: 0 = *never had the experience*, 1 = *almost never*, 2 = *sometimes*, 3 = *almost always*, and 4 = *always*. The functional scale includes statements that describe the impact of the voice disorder on daily activities. The physical scale contains statements representing the client's perceptions of any physical pain or discomfort in and around the larynx as well as of voice quality. The emotional scale elicits information regarding

TABLE 1.2   FUNCTIONAL, PHYSICAL, AND EMOTIONAL CATEGORIES OF QUESTIONS IN THE VOICE HANDICAP INDEX

Functional

My voice makes it difficult for people to hear me.

People have difficulty understanding me in a noisy room.

My family has difficulty hearing me when I call them throughout the house.

I use the phone less often than I would like.

I tend to avoid groups of people because of my voice.

I speak with friends, neighbors, or relatives less often because of my voice.

People ask me to repeat myself when speaking face to face.

My voice difficulties restrict my personal and social life.

I feel left out of conversations because of my voice.

My voice problem causes me to lose income.

Physical

I run out of air when I talk.

The sound of my voice varies throughout the day.

People ask, "What's wrong with your voice?"

My voice sounds creaky and dry.

I feel as though I have to strain to produce voice.

The clarity of my voice is unpredictable.

I try to change my voice to sound different.

I use a great deal of effort to speak.

My voice is worse in the evening.

My voice "gives out" on me in the middle of speaking.

Emotional

I'm tense when talking with others because of my voice.

People seem irritated with my voice.

I find other people don't understand my voice problem.

My voice problem upsets me.

I am less outgoing because of my voice problem.

(*continues*)

TABLE 1.2 *Continued.*

Emotional *Continued*

My voice makes me feel handicapped.

I feel annoyed when people ask me to repeat.

I feel embarrassed when people ask me to repeat.

My voice makes me feel incompetent.

I'm ashamed of my voice problem.

Note. Adapted from "The Voice Handicap Index (VHI): Development and Validation," by B. J. Jacobson, A. Johnson, C. Grywalski, A. Silbergleit, G. Jacobson, M. S. Benninger, et al., 1997, *American Journal of Speech–Language Pathology, 6,* pp. 66–70. Copyright 1997 by American Speech-Language-Hearing Association. Adapted with permission.

the individual's feelings about his or her voice disorder. The higher the VHI score, the greater the client's perception of disability created by the voice problem (Rosen & Murry, 2000). This is currently the most commonly used quality of life measure.

Of the many different ways to assess voice, the most common use auditory–perceptual and instrumental measures. Auditory–perceptual measures are those in which the clinician listens to the individual's voice and makes a subjective determination of the overall level of severity, the appropriateness of the pitch and loudness levels, and the quality of the voice. Instrumental measures include direct and indirect measures of vocal fold structure and function, such as videostrobolaryngoscopy, and measures of acoustic and aerodynamic aspects of vocal function. Although clinicians typically use auditory–perceptual judgments to make an overall decision about the quality of a client's voice and the severity of the problem, most voice clinics also use acoustic, aerodynamic, and physiological instrumentation to evaluate the structure and function of the vocal folds, and the characteristics of the resulting vocal output.

Auditory–Perceptual Evaluation

A formal auditory–perceptual evaluation is an integral part of the diagnostic process. During this portion of the evaluation, the clinician takes the various measures listed below and in Table 1.3.

1. *Maximum phonation time:* The client is asked to take a deep breath and sustain the vowel /a/ for as long as possible. This task is often done at three pitch levels: comfortable pitch, high pitch, and low pitch. This tests the individual's maximum capacity in terms of amount of breath support available for phonation. Adults should be able to sustain voicing for around 20 seconds, and children for 10–15 seconds.
2. *s/z ratio:* The client is asked to take a deep breath and to sustain /s/ for as long as possible, then to do the same for /z/. The time recorded for /s/ is divided by the time recorded for /z/. The normal ratio is around 1.0 to 1.4, indicating that the individual is able to sustain respiration without voicing (/s/) and voicing (/z/) for approximately equal amounts of time. Ratios greater than 1.4 demonstrate that the patient is not able to

TABLE 1.3   MEASURES TAKEN IN AN AUDITORY–PERCEPTUAL EVALUATION

Maximum phonation time

s/z ratio

Pitch range

Endurance

Musculoskeletal tension

Loudness

Presence of hard glottal attack

Cough

Production of reflexive sounds

sustain the voiced sound for as long as the voiceless sound, and may indicate impaired glottal efficiency.

3. *Pitch range:* The client is asked to sing a scale as high and as low as possible. The normal pitch range is around 2.5 to 3 octaves for adults and around 2 octaves for children.

4. *Endurance:* The client is asked to count vigorously to at least 100.

5. *Musculoskeletal tension:* The external laryngeal musculature is palpated by the clinician, and the client identifies points of pain or tenderness.

6. *Loudness:* The client is asked to count while gradually increasing his or her loudness level.

7. *Presence of hard glottal attack:* The client is asked to count from 80 to 90, stopping between each number.

8. *Cough:* The client is asked to cough forcefully. A weak cough often accompanies vocal fold paralysis.

9. *Production of reflexive sounds:* The client is asked to cough, say "uh-huh," laugh, and clear the throat. This is important information for disorders such as spasmodic dysphonia, in which the individual may have normal reflexive vocal function but impaired function for phonation.

Many different types of tests have been developed to perceptually assess the various aspects of voice. Some of the most common are rating scales, semantic differential scales, and visual analog scales. Pitch, loudness, quality, and other vocal features are often rated on equal-appearing interval scales. For example, quality may be rated from 0 to 4, with 0 representing *normal quality* and 4 representing *severely deviant quality*. Table 1.4 presents an example of an equal-appearing rating scale. In semantic differential scales, a series of polar opposites are applied to the person's voice (e.g., normal–abnormal, pleasant–unpleasant, weak–strong, high pitch–low pitch). The evaluator determines where on the continuum between the polar opposites the patient's voice falls, usually on a 7-point scale. Visual analog scales display a horizontal line on which the examiner marks the point that corresponds to the perceived degree of deviance of the designated feature. The American Speech-Language-Hearing Association (2002–2006), for example, developed the Consensus Auditory–Perceptual Evaluation of Voice (CAPE-V) to facilitate communication among professionals by using a set of commonly used and easily understood perceptual vocal attributes: overall severity, roughness, breathiness, strain, pitch, and loudness. The form also indicates whether each attribute appears consistently or inconsistently in the client's speech, and whether additional features are present, such as diplophonia, glottal fry, falsetto, pitch instability, or tremor. Space is also provided for comments regarding the client's resonance characteristics.

Instrumental Measures

Although perceptual measures of voice are valuable in helping the clinician to determine the type and degree of voice abnormality, instrumental measures are also important in a comprehensive voice evaluation. Instrumental measures are useful for identifying the existence of a voice problem, for assessing the severity or stage of progression of the voice problem, for identifying the source of the problem, and as a treatment tool in terms of behavioral modification, biofeedback, or patient education (Stemple et al., 2000). Various types of instruments are used to obtain acoustic, aerodynamic, and physiological measures that greatly expand the scope and depth of the testing process. Instrumentation procedures may provide the clinician with some valuable insight into the way a client is making use of and coordinating the respiratory, phonatory, and articulatory subsystems (Awan, 2001). Instrumental measures also allow the clinician to verify the perceptual aspects of voice. Perceptual judgments alone may not allow for precise tracking of a client's progress, because the ear may not be sensitive

TABLE 1.4 EXAMPLE OF A 5-POINT EQUAL-APPEARING SCALE

	Normal				Severe
	0	1	2	3	4
Breathy (audible escape of air through glottis)					
Vocal fry/creaky (low-frequency periodic vibration)					
Hard glottal attacks (glottal stop at onset of vowels)					
Hyperfunctional/tense (strained or pressed quality)					
Hypofunctional/lax (too little tension in vocal folds; weak, lax, and breathy quality)					
Diplophonia (two different pitches heard simultaneously)					
Voice breaks (intermittent register breaks)					
Grating/harsh (high-pitched noise owing to irregular vocal fold vibrations)					
Rough/coarse (low-pitched noise owing to irregular vocal fold vibrations)					
Unstable voice quality or pitch (irregular variation in quality or pitch)					
Register (mode of phonation: modal, middle, or falsetto)					
Pitch (primary auditory correlate of fundamental frequency)					

Note. Reprinted from *Reference Manual for Communicative Sciences and Disorders,* by R. D. Kent, 1994, Austin, TX: PRO-ED, and from Tables 2 and 3 of "Speech Waveform Perturbation Analysis: A Perceptual-Acoustical Comparison of Seven Measures," by A.G. Askenfelt and B. Hammarberg, 1986, *Journal of Speech and Hearing Research, 29,* p. 54. Adapted with permission of PRO-ED, Inc., and the American Speech-Language-Hearing Association, Rockville, MD.

enough to detect small changes in voice characteristics that indicate the effectiveness of a treatment procedure (Awan, 2001). It is important, however, that the professional using an instrument is knowledgeable about the equipment and skilled in interpreting the information obtained. It is also vital that the device be properly calibrated and maintained in order to collect meaningful data.

Physiological Measures

Physiological measures are used primarily by otolaryngologists to assess vocal fold structure and function. Commonly used measures include indirect laryngoscopy, direct laryngoscopy, endoscopy (flexible or rigid), and videostroboscopy.

Indirect Laryngoscopy

Indirect (mirror) laryngoscopy has been used for many decades to examine the physical structure and function of the vocal folds. In this procedure the client is seated upright, and the laryngologist gently pulls on his or her tongue using a piece of gauze. The examiner then inserts a laryngeal mirror (much like a dental mirror) into the oropharynx region over the tongue. The back of the mirror may actually touch and raise the velum. The examiner wears a headband that has a light attached to it (like a miner's helmet) and focuses the light on the mirror. The examiner sees a mirror image of the vocal folds, which means that the reflection is reversed in terms of left and right. Once the laryngeal reflection is obtained, the client is asked to prolong the /i/ vowel, which helps to raise the epiglottis and expose the vocal folds. Indirect laryngoscopy allows the examiner to detect tissue changes (e.g., nodules and polyps), vocal fold paralysis or weakness, and infections of the larynx (Case, 2002). Normal phonation, however, cannot be visualized.

Direct Laryngoscopy

For direct examination of the larynx, the client must be anesthetized and a laryngoscope placed directly into the throat. With this method, not only can the larynx be visualized in detail, but surgery can be performed with special microlaryngeal instruments that fit through the laryngoscope. Laryngologists and surgeons use laryngoscopic microscopes that allow them to detect tiny changes in tissue structure. Typically, the laryngoscope is also attached to a video so that the image can be enlarged on a screen and recorded. Although this method is more invasive than indirect laryngoscopy, it allows more thorough scrutiny of the laryngeal structures.

Endoscopy and Videostroboscopy

In endoscopic procedures, either a flexible or a rigid endoscope is inserted into the client's pharynx to illuminate the larynx. The procedure may be done via the nose or the mouth. When done via the nose, a very thin, flexible tube is inserted through the nostril into the pharynx. When done via the oral cavity, a rigid scope is inserted. Either way, the illuminated image of the vocal structures is typically projected onto a video screen, using a magnifying scope and video camera. This procedure has many advantages. First, because the client is awake, the risks inherent in general anesthesia are avoided. Second, the procedure allows detailed examination of the structure and function of the larynx. With nasoendoscopy the client is able to phonate relatively normally so that laryngeal movement patterns during phonation can be evaluated. This is particularly important for movement disorders, such as spasmodic dysphonia and paradoxical vocal fold dysfunction, in which the structures look normal but abnormalities in function can be detected.

Often, endoscopic procedures are combined with stroboscopy, allowing evaluation of the movement of the vocal folds during vibration. This technology has become the gold standard of laryngeal evaluation because it allows extensive assessment of both structure and movement patterns of the vocal folds.

Videostroboscopy permits the examiner to visualize many different aspects of vocal fold structure and movement during phonation, including the smoothness of the edges of the vocal folds; the degree to which the vocal folds close; the pattern of vocal fold closure; the extent of opening during abduction; the symmetry of open and closed phases during vibration; the presence and extent of the mucosal wave; the amplitude of vibration; the degree to which both folds reach the midline and point of maximum opening at the same time; the periodicity of a sequence of vibratory cycles; supraglottal activity during phonation; and vertical level of vocal fold approximation (see more detailed list in Table 1.5).

A typical protocol for obtaining and recording vocal fold appearance and movement includes different phonatory and nonphonatory activities to explore the client's vocal mechanism under different circumstances. Tasks include quiet breathing, forced inhalation and exhalation, throat clearing, and vowel production at different levels of pitch and loudness.

Acoustic Analysis

Acoustic analysis of the patient's vocal output is an indirect method of assessing vocal function, as it is not the vocal folds themselves that are observed and analyzed, but the resulting output. From the acoustic analysis, inferences can be made about the way the vocal folds are vibrating. Acoustic analyses are popular because the instrumentation is easily available, is relatively inexpensive, does not require extensive training to use effectively, is safe and noninvasive, and provides visual and quantifiable information that can be used in treatment and for documenting progress in therapy.

TABLE 1.5 VOCAL STRUCTURE AND FUNCTION VISUALIZED BY VIDEOSTROBOSCOPY

Smoothness of vocal fold edge
Normal
Abnormal

Degree of vocal fold closure
Complete
Incomplete
Inconsistent

Patterns of vocal fold closure
Posterior chink
Anterior chink
Hourglass
Bowed
Spindle shaped

Abduction of vocal folds during vibration
Extent of opening
Duration of open and closed phases during vibration

Mucosal wave during vibration
Present
Absent
Extent

Amplitude of vibration
Normal
Less than normal
Greater than normal

Symmetry of vibration
Folds reach midline and maximum opening at the same time
Folds reach midline and maximum opening at different times

Periodicity of vibration
Successive vibrations in a sequence occur with normal regularity
Successive vibrations in a sequence are irregular

Several computerized acoustic devices are available commercially, including the Visi-Pitch and Computerized Speech Lab by Kay Elemetrics, Dr. Speech Science for Windows by Tiger Electronics, and the C-Speech system by Milenkovic. These instruments perform similar types of analyses, including analyses of variables related to fundamental frequency, intensity, and quality and periodicity (see Table 1.6).

Fundamental Frequency

Fundamental frequency (F0) refers to the rate of vibration of the vocal folds and corresponds (although not linearly) to the perceptual domain of pitch. The most common F0 variables measured clinically are average F0 of an isolated vowel; average F0 of a reading or speaking task (often called speaking fundamental frequency, or SFF); frequency range (also called phonational frequency range); and frequency variability, measured as the standard deviation of F0.

TABLE 1.6   ACOUSTIC MEASURES OF VOCAL OUTPUT

Fundamental frequency (F0)

Average F0 of vowel

Average F0 of connected speech (speaking F0)

Frequency variability

Maximum phonational frequency range

Intensity

Average intensity

Dynamic range

Quality/periodicity

Jitter

Shimmer

Harmonics-to-noise ratio/noise-to-harmonics ratio

Average Fundamental Frequency

Average F0 is helpful in comparing a client's F0 to norms that have been established for men, women, and children. As a rough guideline, the average F0 for adult males is around 100–120 Hz, the average for adult females is 180–230 Hz, and the average for children is 250–300 Hz. However, it is well established that even in adulthood F0 changes with increasing age, declining for older women and increasing for older men. Quantifying a speaker's F0 levels and making comparisons with established norms for speakers of similar age and gender will help the clinician decide whether a perceived pitch abnormality really does result from an F0 problem or whether other vocal factors are involved (Ferrand, 2007).

Maximum Phonational Frequency Range

Maximum phonational frequency range (MPFR) refers to the extent of F0s the speaker can produce from lowest to highest, and this value can also be compared to appropriate norms. MPFR reflects the physiological limits of an individual's voice (Colton et al., 2006). It is expressed either in hertz or in octaves or in semitones. Ferrand (2007) reported that most normal speakers have a range of around 2.5 octaves or 30 semitones. Colton et al. (2006) noted that the lowest frequency adult males are able to produce is around 80 Hz, and the highest is in the 700-Hz range. Adult females produce a low F0 of approximately 135 Hz and a high of over 1000 Hz. Clinically, it has been found that physical condition affects phonational frequency range more than either age or gender; that is, older speakers in good health tend to have a larger range than younger speakers in poor health.

Frequency Variability

Frequency variability is measured either in hertz, as the standard deviation of F0, or in semitones (called "pitch sigma").

This variable can be used as an index of vocal fold vibration stability or as a measure of intonational appropriateness. That is, when a person sustains an isolated vowel, the standard deviation of F0 should be small, indicating good control of the muscles involved in pitch regulation. On the other hand, during connected speech the standard deviation of F0 should be larger, reflecting the increases and decreases in F0 that are characteristic of linguistic intonational patterns of a language. People constantly change their F0 levels as they speak to reflect different emotions, different types of accenting and stress of syllables, and different grammatical constructions. These F0 changes contribute to the overall melody, or prosody, of speech. A certain amount of frequency variability is desirable in a speaker's voice, depending on the individual's age, gender, social situation, mood, dialect, and other internal and external factors. This variability is something that speakers of a particular language in a particular culture intuitively recognize. Too much or too little frequency variability sounds wrong and can indicate a functional, organic, or neurogenic voice problem (Ferrand, 2007). Standard deviation of F0 in normal conversational speech is around 20–35 Hz (Ferrand, 2007). In terms of pitch sigma, the value should be around 2–4 semitones (Colton et al., 2006).

Intensity Measures

Intensity corresponds perceptually to loudness. Like F0, intensity can be measured in terms of average intensity of an isolated vowel or connected speech, intensity variability, and intensity range (usually called dynamic range). Intensity can be measured with commercially available acoustic instruments or by means of a sound-level meter, easily available from electronics stores. While norms for frequency are plentiful, those for intensity are not. However, normal conversational speech typically ranges around 55–75 dB SPL. Lower or higher levels may also be used, depending on the situation. Obviously, someone whispering in a classroom would want to use a lower intensity level than when he or she is cheering for a favorite sports team. Maximum intensity levels are reportedly around 100–110 dB SPL, and minimum levels not involving whispering are around 40 dB SPL (Colton et al., 2006; Kent, 1994). To obtain the dynamic range, the examiner asks the person to say "ah" as softly as possible and as loudly as possible, at a comfortable frequency level. In terms of dynamic range, a value of approximately 30 dB SPL indicates normal voice function for adults (Rammage, Morrison, & Nichol, 2001).

Quality and Periodicity

Jitter, shimmer, and harmonics-to-noise ratio (HNR) are acoustic measures used to quantify aspects of vocal quality and vocal fold periodicity. These types of analyses are typically included in commercially available instruments. *Jitter,* which refers to variation in frequency across individual cycles of vibration, is measured in percent or in milliseconds (msec). *Shimmer,* or the variation in amplitude across individual cycles of vibration, is measured in decibels or in percent. *HNR* refers to the ratio of harmonic (periodic) components in the voice to inharmonic (noise) components, and is measured in decibels. Various researchers have reported norms for these measures. In general, the level of jitter in the normal human voice is around 0.2%–1.0%, shimmer is 0.5 dB or less, and HNR should be at least around 10 dB. The higher the level of jitter and/or shimmer in the person's voice, the less periodically the vocal folds are vibrating. On the other hand, the higher the HNR, the more harmonic elements and fewer inharmonic elements are evident in the vocal output.

These measures are useful in detecting subtle aspects of laryngeal function that may not be auditorily perceptible but that indicate some kind of problem in vocal fold vibration. Measures such as these are also used widely as a baseline before treatment and to document changes in the client's vocal output following behavioral, medical, and surgical interventions.

Aerodynamic Measures

Aerodynamic measures quantify air volumes and airflows used for voice production purposes. Vocal fold vibration results from the interaction between muscular and elastic forces (the vocal folds), subglottal pressure, and airflow through the glottis. Measurements of air volumes and airflows therefore reflect the client's ability to use the laryngeal mechanism effectively in regulating the flow of air for phonation. Table 1.7 lists the most commonly used aerodynamic measures.

Air Volume

Various measures of volume are relevant to voice production, including vital capacity (VC) and tidal volume (TV). VC refers to the total amount of air that an individual is able to use voluntarily. The measurement involves inhaling the maximum amount of air possible and then exhaling maximally into a spirometer. VC varies according to age, gender, and build, but on average is around 5,000 ml. TV refers to the amount of air inhaled and exhaled per breath. For normal quiet breathing TV is around 10% of VC, or

---

TABLE 1.7   AERODYNAMIC MEASURES AND PHONATORY/RESPIRATORY EFFICIENCY

Air volume

Airflow rate

Subglottal pressure

Maximum phonation time

s/z ratio

---

approximately 500 ml. Normal conversational speech typically falls within 20% of VC, or 1,000 ml per breath for speech. Because normal speech requires only a small percentage of VC, patients with a somewhat limited VC may not be affected in terms of voice. However, a patient with a greatly reduced vital capacity may demonstrate short maximum phonation times, short speech phrases, and a weak voice with reduced intensity due to difficulty achieving adequate subglottal pressure during speech (Koschkee & Rammage, 1997).

Airflow Rate

Airflow rate refers to the rate at which air passes through the glottis during phonation. It is measured in milliliters per second using a device called a pneumotachograph. This device requires the individual to phonate into a face mask attached to a pressure sensor, and the pressure is converted into an electrical signal so it can be displayed. The larynx is an important regulator of airflow for voice production. If the larynx allows too much air to flow through the glottis during vocalization, the patient's voice will be breathy. On the other hand, if the vocal folds are closed too tightly, allowing too little air through the glottis, the voice will be tense and strained (Ferrand, 2007).

Average airflow rates of approximately 80–200 ml/sec have been reported as normal (Stemple et al., 2000). Stemple et al. noted that speakers with glottal incompetence due to problems such as vocal fold paralysis may generate average airflow rates as high as 400–600 ml/sec, accompanied by short vowel durations. Individuals with severely hyperfunctional voice or glottal fry will demonstrate markedly reduced airflow rates, as low as 10–15 ml/sec.

Subglottal Air Pressure

Subglottal air pressure (P_s) is usually not measured directly, because to do so involves inserting a measurement device into the trachea. Rather, pressure is indirectly estimated from a client's production of a stop sound such as /p/. The rationale for this procedure is that for the voiceless stop sound, the lips are closed and the vocal folds are open, so that the pressures in the oral cavity and subglottal area are approximately equal. Thus, pressure can be obtained orally, reflecting the pressure within the trachea. A tube in the individual's mouth is attached to a pressure transducer, and he or she produces a series of /pi/ syllables. For normal conversational speech, the subglottal pressure is around 5–10 cm H_2O. Pressure requirements are higher to produce a louder voice and also vary depending on F0. Higher frequencies, with increased vocal fold tension, need more P_S, whereas lower frequencies, with vocal folds that are more lax, require less P_S in order to be set into vibration.

Phonatory and Respiratory Efficiency

A client's glottal efficiency during phonation and his or her ability to effectively control the forces of expiration (elastic muscle force, rib recoil, lung tissue pressure, gravity) should be assessed during the voice evaluation. One common method for assessment is the measure of maximum phonation time, or the length of time the person is able to sustain a vowel on one breath. When respiratory function is compromised, an individual will either experience a reduction in the amount of air available to support phonation or have a problem controlling the airflow (Colton et al., 2006). Very young children have been reported to sustain a vowel for just under 10 seconds. Adult men typically can sustain a vowel for more than 20 seconds and adult women for just under 20 seconds (Kent, 1994).

A variant of maximum phonation time is the *s/z* ratio. This simple clinical test measures the difference in time that a client can sustain a voiceless sound compared to a voiced sound. A person with normal vocal production should be able to sustain both voiceless and voiced sounds for approximately equal amounts of time, resulting in a ratio of

1.0. The ratio is obtained by dividing the duration of the /s/ by the duration of the /z/. If the individual sustains /s/ for 20 seconds and /z/ for 20 seconds, dividing 20 into 20 results in a ratio of 1.0. If the respiratory system is compromised and the laryngeal system is intact, there should be an equal reduction in expiratory airflow for the voiceless /s/ and the voiced /z/, which would also yield a ratio approximating 1.0 (Colton et al., 2006). For example, if the client sustains both /s/ and /z/ for 10 seconds, the ratio would still be 1.0. However, if the individual has normal respiratory support but problems with vocal fold vibration, the /s/ should be prolonged normally whereas air wastage will likely occur during the voiced /z/. This pattern results in a ratio greater than 1.0. For example, if the person holds the /s/ for 20 seconds but the /z/ for only 10 seconds, a ratio of 2.0 is obtained. Based on research, a ratio above around 1.4 is considered to be an indication of abnormal laryngeal valving.

Chapter 2
Structural Disorders

Structural disorders refer to changes in the tissues of the larynx and vocal folds or changes in laryngeal functioning, and can occur for a wide variety of reasons including phonotrauma (vocal abuse and misuse), congenital or acquired conditions, injury, disease, and developmental and maturational factors. Tissue changes can interfere not only with phonation, but with breathing and swallowing as well. Some of the relatively more common structural disorders include nodules, polyps, contact ulcers, papillomas, subglottic stenosis, laryngeal web, sulcus vocalis, cysts, and laryngomalacia. Some structural disorders are listed in Table 2.1.

Changes to the vocal folds such as nodules, polyps, and contact ulcers with or without granulomas are typically,

TABLE 2.1   SELECTED STRUCTURAL DISORDERS OF THE LARYNX

Nodules

Polyps

Ulcers/granuloma

Cysts

Sulcus vocalis

Papilloma

Subglottic stenosis

Laryngeal web

Laryngomalacia

but not always, related to phonotrauma (i.e., abuse of the voice). Phonotrauma tends to be associated with lifestyle and personality factors, such as participation in activities that require excessive vocal output (e.g., debate team, cheerleading). People who use their voices professionally, such as teachers, singers, and aerobics instructors, are particularly prone to nodules. Smoking is extremely vocally abusive, but any type of abuse (excessive talking, talking over noise, poor vocal technique in singing, excessive throat clearing, chronic cough, etc.) can irritate and inflame the sensitive tissues of the vocal folds. With continued trauma, the inflammation and swelling can localize and histological changes can take place, generating a nodule, polyp, or ulcer. Often, many factors interact and create the voice problem. A person who talks a lot may also sing in a choir, smoke, be under stress at work, and suffer from gastric reflux. All these factors can combine to create the conditions for laryngeal tissue changes to occur.

Nodules

Nodules are benign growths that develop on the epithelium of the vocal folds as a consequence of vocal hyperfunction and resulting inflammation of the folds. The growths typically occur at the point where vocal fold vibration is most vigorous and the folds collide with the greatest force during vibration. This point is at the junction between the anterior one third and posterior two thirds of the vocal folds, which is the midpoint of the membranous glottis. Nodules are often bilateral, as the growth on one fold irritates the corresponding spot on the opposite fold. Nodules begin as soft reddish growths, filled with fluid. Over time and with continued hyperfunction, they harden and become whitish due to fibrosis (formation of fibrous tissue as a healing process) and thickening of the epithelium.

Nodules are strongly related to vocal hyperfunction and trauma. They may be caused by any vocal behavior that irritates the vocal folds and results in inflammation, such as talking too much, talking too loudly, screaming and yelling, habitual coughing or throat clearing, singing, smoking, and so on. Conditions such as acid reflux can also contribute to the formation of nodules. Individuals with vocal nodules do not relax their laryngeal muscles properly, keeping the muscles in a tense state during both adduction and abduction (Pontes, Kyrillos, Behlau, De Biase, & Pontes, 2002). Videolaryngostroboscopy shows that the larynx is often abnormally contracted from front to back. The arytenoid cartilages are pulled forward, and there may be an open space or chink at the back of the glottis related to the increased tension of the thyroarytenoid muscle (Pontes et al., 2002).

The vocal symptoms of nodules range from mild to severe, and typically include different degrees of hoarseness and breathiness, and sometimes a lowered pitch. The nodules prevent the vocal folds from closing completely along their length, resulting in gaps that allow air to leak out. The growths also interfere with the mucosal wave, resulting in aperiodic vibration and the perception of noise and hoarseness. Because of the increased mass of the vocal fold with the addition of the nodule, fundamental frequency (F0) may be lowered, with the corresponding perception of lowered pitch. Often, clients report that their voice quality is best early in the morning and deteriorates as the day progresses.

The best treatment for nodules is behavioral voice therapy, focusing on vocal education, vocal hygiene, and improved vocal usage. Occasionally, nodules will not resolve, even when the individual is compliant with the therapy regimen, in which case surgery may be necessary to remove the growth. In children, however, surgery is seldom recommended, for two reasons. First, without removing the vocally abusive patterns, the growth is likely to recur. Second, the nodules often resolve spontaneously in children, particularly in boys. In adults, the decision whether to operate is less clear. See Chapter 7 for a detailed description of a typical vocal hygiene and vocal abuse reduction program.

Polyps

Similar to nodules, *polyps* are also benign growths on the vocal folds that may result from hyperfunction. However, polyps are filled with fluid and tend to be softer than mature nodules. Although nodules are typically bilateral, polyps are more commonly unilateral. Polyps are not confined to a particular location on the vocal folds; they may occur at subglottal, glottal, or supraglottal levels. In addition, whereas nodules occur over time with continued vocal hyperfunction, polyps may occur with just one episode of extreme vocal abuse. Polyps may also occur due to infection, allergies, gastroesophageal reflux, and endocrine disorders such as hypothyroidism. Table 2.2 summarizes the differences between nodules and polyps.

Polyps may be pedunculated with a thin, stalk-like base, or sessile with a broad, flat base. Polypoid degeneration, also called Reinke's edema, is a condition in which the entire vocal fold is affected, rather than the lesion being localized to one spot. The entire membranous portion of the vocal folds becomes infiltrated with thick, gelatinous fluid, giving them the appearance of enlarged, fluid-filled bags or balloons (Stemple, Glaze, & Klaben, 2000). The condi-

TABLE 2.2 DIFFERENCES BETWEEN NODULES AND POLYPS	
Nodules	**Polyps**
Typically bilateral	Typically unilateral
Typically sessile	May be sessile, pedunculated, or degenerative
Mature over time	May occur from one episode of trauma
Occur at the midpoint of the membranous glottis	May occur at subglottal, glottal, or supraglottal locations

tion varies in severity but typically is associated with heavy smoking. Phonation has been reported to be effortful, and individuals with this vocal problem may also have difficulty breathing on exertion because of the enlarged bulk of the vocal folds (Mathieson, 2001). Symptoms vary depending on the extent and location of the polyp. If the polyp interferes with vocal fold closure and vibration, dysphonia will result. Typically, the dysphonia is characterized by a hoarse and breathy quality, as well as a low pitch.

Behavioral voice treatment alone may or may not be effective for polyps. Surgery is often required. Even with surgery, however, voice therapy is essential to prevent the polyp from recurring. In addition, before undergoing surgery, the individual needs to take care of any other contributing factors such as smoking and gastroesophageal reflux. If the polyp or polypoid degeneration persists despite such efforts, surgery should then be considered. Surgery involves removing the gelatinous material with gentle dissection and/or suction.

Contact Ulcers and Granulomas

An *ulcer* is a lesion on a mucosal surface caused by superficial loss of tissue and usually occurs in conjunction with inflammation. A *granuloma* refers to a mass of tissue consisting of inflammation, a large number of blood cells, and connective tissue covered by squamous epithelium (Garnett, 2005a). Contact ulcers occur on the posterior cartilaginous part of the vocal folds, where the folds attach to the vocal processes of the arytenoid cartilages. A lesion may be unilateral or bilateral. Although the lesion is located in the back portion of the glottis, the anterior sections may also look unhealthy, with thickening of the cover (Mathieson, 2001). The tissue on the arytenoid cartilages looks swollen and inflamed. Contact granulomas may be pedunculated or sessile, and may vary in color from pale to red (Garnett,

2005a). The ulcers occur when the mucosa covering the vocal processes collides repeatedly with the opposite cartilage. Because the mucosa is thin and delicate, and overlies the less flexible cartilage, it is crushed between any unyielding object (e.g., an endotracheal tube or the opposite arytenoid cartilage) and the cartilage beneath it. This causes the mucosa to break down, creating the ulcer and resulting in the formation of the granuloma.

The primary cause of contact ulcers is vocal abuse, particularly the use of an extremely low pitch in conjunction with an effortful voice quality. The configuration of the glottis for such vocal use causes the vocal processes to collide with excessive force, and over time the mucosal breakdown results in ulceration and granulation. Another cause of contact ulcers is gastroesophageal reflux. The acidic stomach contents backflow up the esophagus and into the pharyngeal and laryngeal areas. The acidity irritates and inflames the sensitive laryngeal tissues in the posterior part of the larynx. Lack of adequate hydration can worsen this condition. Endotracheal intubation can also cause contact ulcers. Whenever an individual has a general anesthetic, a breathing tube is inserted through the larynx. The tube can exert pressure against the vocal folds, particularly in the posterior region, and create ulceration. Individuals who need to be ventilated for long periods of time tend to be prone to contact ulcers. Other factors that have been implicated in the formation of ulcers and granuloma include smoking, allergies, infections, postnasal drip, and chronic throat clearing (Garnett, 2005a). Because some individuals experience more than one of these conditions (e.g., vocal abuse, acid reflux, postnasal drip), it is important to treat all of the potential causes.

Unlike other benign tumors, such as nodules and polyps, contact ulcers are painful. The pain may occur as a burning sensation in the larynx or as a shooting pain in the ear (Mathieson, 2001). The pain may be particularly acute when the individual coughs or clears his or her throat (Garnett,

2005a). In terms of voice production, there is some controversy. Stemple et al. (2000) noted that vocal fold vibration is not affected unless there is also a large granuloma. However, they also commented that many clients do complain of restricted pitch ranges and voice fatigue. Garnett (2005a) stated that symptoms include varying degrees of hoarseness, and a low-pitched, pressed voice quality, as well as cough, throat clearing, and a rough foreign body sensation. Garnett noted that even if the client does not show symptoms, the ulcer and/or granuloma should be treated to prevent possible complications, including airway obstruction, vocal fold fixation, and posterior laryngeal stenosis.

Correct diagnosis of the cause or causes of the ulcer is essential so the appropriate treatment plan can be developed. A thorough voice evaluation by a speech–language pathologist is critical, in order to assess the type and amount of vocally abusive behaviors, including poor breath support, hard glottal attack, and inappropriate pitch levels. In addition, it is important for professionals to evaluate other factors that may be contributing to the problem (acid reflux, allergies, etc.). Treatment usually focuses on the causes of the problem, and therefore voice therapy is essential to reduce or eliminate the abuse. It is critical to treat acid reflux, allergies, postnasal drip, and so forth. According to Garnett (2005a), most clients whose underlying cause of ulcer is vocal abuse respond well to speech therapy and medical management, and most individuals whose underlying cause is reflux respond well to medical management. Surgery is rarely indicated because there are some problems with surgical management (Garnett, 2005a): the recurrence rate after surgery is high, around 37%–50%, and the surgery may cause the granuloma to migrate along the edge of the wound. However, when the ulcer does not respond to improved diet and voice therapy, one option is Botox injection in conjunction with speech therapy. The Botox is injected into the thyroarytenoid muscle on the same side as the granuloma, with the aim of weakening the muscle

(De Biase, Master, Pontes, & De Biase, 2001). This prevents the vocal folds from slamming together with excessive force; in other words, it is a chemical means of inducing a much less abusive glottal attack. With voice therapy, the patient is taught to produce a gentle onset of phonation when full use of the muscle returns (see Chapter 7).

Laryngeal Cysts

Cysts, which are sacs filled with fluid, typically occur when glandular secretions and mucus accumulate and are unable to dissipate due to blockage of the sac. The inner surface of the cyst is lined with mucus. Laryngeal cysts can occur in any structure in the larynx where mucous glands are present (Moorhead, 2006), including the true and false vocal folds. Cysts may be congenital or acquired. Some types of acquired cysts may be associated with laryngeal cancer, so it is important that the client be referred for a laryngeal examination to rule out the possibility of malignancy. When a cyst occurs within the true vocal fold, typically the cyst is firmly stuck to the underlying vocal ligament, but not to the overlying tissue of the superficial layer of the lamina propria. Cysts are usually sessile; that is, they have a broad base. They may be unilateral or bilateral, and may give rise to thickening of the tissue of the opposite fold because of the constant irritation (Stemple et al., 2000). The most common symptoms of cysts in adults are hoarseness, pain, dysphagia, and the feeling of a foreign body (Moorhead, 2006).

Cysts are usually excised surgically, either endoscopically with a laser if the mass is small enough, or through an external procedure, such as a lateral thyrotomy, for a larger cyst. In a thyrotomy the thyroid cartilage is divided vertically, and the cyst is cut out through this incision. Needle aspiration used to be advocated as a safe and fairly noninvasive procedure, but the cyst tends to recur with this method. Tracheotomy may be necessary for infants with cysts that block the airway, causing severe respiratory distress.

Sulcus Vocalis

Sulcus vocalis refers to a groove or indentation along the medial edge of one or both vocal folds. The groove may be shallow (confined to the cover of the folds) or deep (extending into the vocal ligament). The cause of the problem has not been conclusively established, but it seems that it can be either congenital or acquired. Stemple et al. (2000) reported that one theory to explain congenital sulcus is that the groove emerges due to abnormal maturation of the vocal fold cover in embryologic development. Patients with congenital sulci typically have a lifelong history of disordered voice (Schweinfurth & Ossoff, 2001). Causes of acquired sulcus include changes in the tissues of the vocal folds resulting from aging, vocal fold paralysis, infection, and degeneration of benign lesions (Schweinfurth & Ossoff, 2001). Laryngeal surgery can also result in the formation of a sulcus. Stripping of the vocal folds used to be done for polypoid degeneration, but it is now known that this kind of procedure, in which the deeper layers of the vocal fold are invaded, facilitates the formation of a sulcus, with the associated scarring that occurs.

Diagnosis of sulcus must be done with laryngovideostroboscopy, because this condition cannot be seen on indirect laryngoscopy. With videostroboscopy, it can be seen that the groove in the fold has the effect of tethering the lamina propria at the site of the sulcus (Mathieson, 2001), and thus interfering with the mucosal wave. In addition, the vocal folds often appear bowed. According to Schweinfurth and Ossoff (2001), the mucosa in the area of the sulcus is scarred down to the vocal ligament, giving the fold a retracted appearance. Symptoms range in severity, but typically the client's voice is hoarse and weak. Often, speakers experience vocal fatigue because of the degree of effort required to produce voice. In less severe cases, however, the voice may sound essentially normal, with the main symptoms being vocal fatigue or a decreased range in singing (Schweinfurth & Ossoff, 2001).

Treatment is usually surgical, involving the freeing up of the affected area from the vocal ligament so the fold can vibrate without interference. Another approach is injection of a biocompatible material, such as collagen or fat, between the vocal ligament and cover or within the layers of the lamina propria to compensate for the lost tissue. This improves the flexibility of the cover (Schweinfurth & Ossoff, 2001). This technique may also help to prevent further scar formation in the deeper layers of the folds. Thick bands of scar tissue may be removed surgically. Medialization procedures such as Type I thyroplasty (see Chapter 7) may be effective in facilitating vocal fold closure to improve the patient's volume and projection of voice. Also, any concurrent problems that affect voice (e.g., reflux, allergies) need to be treated. Behavioral voice therapy is also important, to teach the person to reduce hyperfunctional voice patterns, both before and after surgery. It is crucial to teach the client good vocal hygiene before surgery, both to reduce further trauma to the folds before surgery and to produce the best results possible after surgery. Speech therapy is also useful to teach the individual how to use the voice most efficiently in order to reduce vocal fatigue.

Papillomas

Papillomas are small, warty, benign tumors that can be sessile or pedunculated. Although benign, the tumors can spread and cause severe complications in terms of both voice and swallowing. Papillomas can occur in children and adults, and the disease is usually more severe and aggressive in children. The growths tend to begin at the anterior portion of the vocal folds, on the epithelium, but can spread all over the vocal folds, into the vocal ligament and the vocalis muscle and even further to the false and aryepiglottic folds, trachea, and bronchi. The symptoms depend on the location and severity of the tumors. Common symptoms are hoarseness and breathiness, with aphonia occurring less frequently. In addition, when the person's airway is obstructed, stridor and dyspnea may be present. At first, stridor may occur only during inspiration, but as the disease progresses, stridor may occur during both phases of breathing. The individual may also develop a cough, pneumonia, and dysphagia.

The cause of the disease is the human papillomavirus (HPV). This is a large family of viruses that causes diseases such as genital warts and cervical cancer. Laryngeal papillomas are caused by HPV 6 and HPV 11. The childhood form of the disease may be caused during the birth process when the baby's upper aerodigestive tract is exposed to the mother's genital HPV (McClay, 2006). However, not all babies born to infected mothers will develop laryngeal papillomas. Other factors, such as the status of the baby's immune system, length of time in the birth canal, and amount of virus in the birth canal, may contribute to the development or lack of development of the disease. Laryngeal papillomas in adults may result from sexual transmission of the virus (Harman, 2002; McClay, 2006).

The goals of treatment include reducing the papillomas, creating a safe airway, improving voice quality, and increasing the time interval between surgical procedures (McClay, 2006). Because of the aggressiveness of the disease, repeated surgeries are the norm, with particularly severe cases sometimes requiring removal as often as every 2–4 weeks. These frequent surgeries can have secondary consequences, such as scarring or webbing of the vocal folds, and even the development of subglottic stenosis.

Most otolaryngologists remove the papillomas by CO_2 laser, although if the tumors are very large and extensive, surgical removal using microlaryngeal techniques may be performed first to get rid of much of the growth. In addition, reducing the extent of the tumors may help to encourage remission of the disease. However, even when all the lesions have been removed, the virus may remain in a latent state in surrounding tissues, and this may explain why the disease can recur. Tracheotomy should be avoided if possible, as there have been reports that this can result in even more extensive spread of the disease or cause the tumors to become cancerous (Eicher, 1991). Harman (2002) noted, however, that 10%–15% of children with severe laryngeal papillomas do require tracheotomy, and that the papillomas will become malignant in 3%–5% of these patients.

In addition to surgical removal of the growths, many patients and their families have turned to nonsurgical therapies, including antiviral, hormonal, immunological, and chemotherapeutic procedures (Stern, 2001). For example, some people are treated with interferon, which is a naturally produced protein with antiviral and antitumor actions that can also modify immune system reactions (Harman, 2002). Another type of nonsurgical therapy is the use of Indole-3-carbinol. This compound, found in vegetables such as cabbage, broccoli, and cauliflower, and also sold in health food stores, acts hormonally and has been shown to decrease laryngeal papillomas in mice. Cydofovir, an antiviral agent used in papilloma treatment, is absorbed into cells and then kills off cells with HPV while not affecting normal cells (Stern, 2001). It is usually injected either directly into the lesions or into the places where the lesions were removed during surgery (Harman, 2002; Stern, 2001). These types of therapies may lengthen the intervals between surgeries. Behavioral voice therapy may be appropriate after surgical removal of papillomas to help the individual make the best possible use of his or her vocal mechanism. For example, vocal function exercises in which the client phonates different vowels while gliding up and down his or her pitch range may reduce the stiffness of the vocal folds (see Chapter 7). A program of vocal education also may be appropriate. The clinician can help the client to identify any vocal abuses and explore strategies to eliminate them, as well as practice techniques to optimize effective communication. If the client is a smoker, the clinician should strongly discourage smoking.

Subglottic Stenosis

Stenosis refers to the narrowing or constricting of an orifice. The laryngeal airway can be narrowed along any point, but stenosis is most common in the subglottic cricoid area, below the true vocal folds, because that is the narrowest and least expandable point of the airway. *Subglottic stenosis*, therefore, usually refers to a narrowing of the airway between the glottis and the first tracheal ring (Deem & Miller, 2000). Depending on the cause of the problem, the major symptom will typically be stridor. Subglottic stenosis can be either congenital or acquired through various causes, such as infection, gastroesophageal reflux disease (GERD), abnormal tissue growth, diseases, and, most commonly, endotracheal intubation.

Congenital Subglottic Stenosis (CSS)

CSS occurs from some kind of problem during embryological development, resulting in either a thickened or deformed cricoid cartilage or a thickening of the tissues that line the inside of the cartilage. The severity of the condition depends on the extent of the narrowing. For instance, in a mild case, the child may not usually exhibit any symptoms. However, if the child has an upper respiratory infection, the added edema in conjunction with the narrowed airway might produce more severe airway obstruction. A child with a more severe case will present with more symptoms, such as stridor on both inhalation and exhalation, in addition to a hoarse or weak voice. Most children outgrow the condition, but depending on the cause and whether there are any related problems, some individuals will need surgical and/or pharmacological treatment with antibiotics, corticosteroids, and reflux medication.

Acquired Subglottic Stenosis (ASS)

ASS may be the result of numerous causes, including infection, disease, and intubation. Endotracheal intubation, either during anesthesia or in long-term cases, is the most prevalent cause of ASS, accounting for around 90% of all cases (Garnett, 2005b). The respiratory epithelium is very susceptible to irritation and swelling, and the pressure of the endotracheal tube against the delicate tissue may result in swelling and irritation (Santer & D'Alessandro, n.d.), which can then lead to ulceration and growth of granulation tissue. If the individual suffers from gastric reflux, this can further worsen the problem. The tissues surrounding the cartilage and the cartilage itself can become inflamed, eventually collapsing. Healing can result in scarring, which, together with the weakened cartilage, narrows or completely closes the lumen.

The severity of the obstruction determines the type of treatment. Mild cases can usually be treated endoscopically with CO_2 laser, whereas more severe obstruction needs to be treated surgically. Surgical techniques focus on removing the obstruction, enlarging the airway, and maintaining a functional voice. A type of surgical treatment called laryngotracheal reconstruction involves making a slit in the cricoid cartilage and grafting cartilage from the patient's ear or rib into the slit to widen the airway. Laryngotracheal reconstruction can affect the resulting voice by influencing the position and movement of the vocal folds (Andrews, 1995). For instance, a graft in the anterior portion of the cricoid may inhibit the action of the cricothyroid muscles, thus influencing pitch regulation. On the other hand, a graft in the posterior cricoid region widens the posterior glottis. This can affect the functioning of the interarytenoid muscles, resulting in incomplete vocal fold closure during vibration. Thus, voice quality after these types of reconstructive surgeries is often breathy, weak, and rough. When reflux is present, it should be treated before surgery is attempted in order to increase the chance of success.

Laryngeal Web

A *laryngeal web* is a sheet of connective tissue between the vocal folds. Typically, webs are located at the anterior commissure and vary in length and thickness. A web can be so small that the person is unaware of its presence or so extensive that it causes severe airway obstruction. Occasionally, the web completely obliterates the glottis, a congenital condition known as laryngeal atresia. Immediate removal of the web is critical in this case.

Webs can be congenital or acquired. Congenital webs are rare, making up about 5% of laryngeal anomalies (Lee, 2001). Most webs are acquired from some kind of trauma that irritates and inflames the vocal folds. Webs acquired due to intubation trauma typically occur on the middle or posterior portion of the folds (Andrews, 1995). Webs acquired following laryngeal surgeries are usually very small, and are called microwebs or synechias. These webs occur when the anterior commissure is irritated and then heals. According to Lee (2001), 75% of webs are located at the level of the vocal folds and the remainder are supraglottal or transglottal. Depending on the extent of the web, the individual may be aphonic or hoarse and stridor may be present. Feeding problems may also occur (Lee, 2001).

The simplest surgical treatment is dilation of the web. *Dilation* refers to enlarging an opening or the lumen of a hollow structure. Dilation involves dividing the web using a bronchoscope (Lee, 2001). However, the procedure itself can result in the formation of scar tissue. Other ways of dividing the web include the use of scissors, knife, or CO_2 laser. Another surgical procedure used on webs is *lysis,* which is the surgical division of adhesions. Endoscopic lysis by itself also has not been very successful in treating thick webs. A treatment that works better for thick webs is an anterior thyrotomy together with lysis. In this procedure, rather than gaining access to the web via an endoscope, the surgeon cuts the front portion of the thyroid cartilage and divides the web surgically from that position. Then a keel, usually made of silicon, is inserted between the folds and kept in place for 3–6 weeks. This is done to keep the folds separated to prevent them from healing with a new web. However, there are a few drawbacks to this technique. First, because it is an open procedure rather than an endoscopic one, it is more invasive as it involves cutting of structures. Second, the keel must be removed surgically once healing has occurred. Another disadvantage is that after the keel is removed, a temporary tracheotomy may be necessary to ensure that the patient has a functioning airway.

Laryngomalacia

Laryngomalacia, a congenital disorder, refers to a condition in which the supraglottal cartilages of the larynx are excessively flexible, resulting in a characteristically elongated epiglottis. The vocal folds, however, are not affected, so phonation tends to be unimpaired. The primary problem is respiratory, due to the fact that upon inhalation the aryepiglottic folds are sucked inward. This can obstruct the airway, resulting in inspiratory stridor with a high-pitched, harsh quality. The stridor becomes worse when the child cries, exerts him- or herself, is laid on his or her back, is feeding or excited, or has an upper respiratory infection.

Most children grow out of this condition by age 3 or 4 years and typically do not require therapy. However, around 10%–15 % of babies with this disorder need surgery to improve their airway (Giannoni, 1994). When the airway is severely compromised, not only is respiration affected, but the child may not be able to feed properly, so growth and development are affected (Rammage et al., 2001). Complications that can result when the disorder is very severe include cyanosis (a condition in which the skin turns blue or purplish due to a lack of oxygen), retraction of the chest wall, and even heart failure.

Although laryngomalacia can occur in isolation, it sometimes occurs in conjunction with other problems, such as tracheomalacia (collapse of the tracheal walls), vocal fold paralysis, weakness of the pharyngeal muscles, and gastroesophageal reflux disease (GERD). In fact, GERD has been documented in around 80% of patients with laryngomalacia (Giannoni, 1994). If GERD is present, it is important to treat the reflux before any surgery is performed. If the reflux is not treated, the condition can persist after the surgery.

Different types of surgery are available to treat this condition. One procedure is to fixate the epiglottis to prevent it from being pulled inward upon inhalation. Another procedure is laser removal of tissue to enlarge the airway. A technique that is currently popular is the CO_2 laser supraglottoplasty technique, in which the aryepiglottic folds are divided and the excess arytenoid tissue is vaporized (Giannoni, 1994). In rare instances in which the condition is life threatening, the child may require a tracheotomy to establish an airway.

Chapter 3
Inflammation and Irritation of the Larynx

This chapter focuses on acute and chronic forms of laryngitis, including laryngeal inflammations caused by compromised immune systems and autoimmune disorders such as rheumatoid arthritis. Also discussed is a disorder known variously as irritable larynx syndrome, paradoxical vocal fold motion, and paradoxical vocal fold disorder, among other names. The chapter concludes with information regarding chronic cough.

Laryngitis

The term *laryngitis* is an umbrella term, covering any inflammation of the larynx. *Inflammation* refers to cellular and chemical reactions that occur in blood vessels and adjacent tissues in response to injury or abnormal stimulation. Inflamed tissues are typically swollen and edematous. The inflammation can be infectious or noninfectious, chronic or acute. In severe cases it can obstruct the airway. Laryngitis affects individuals of all ages, but is often more of a problem in infants and young children than in adults, because of their much smaller larynx. Swelling of the laryngeal tissues may create airway obstruction in a small larynx, whereas the same amount of swelling in a larger larynx would have minimal effects.

There are numerous causes of laryngitis, including viral infections (influenza, measles, mumps, chicken pox), bacterial infections, vocal abuse, smoking, allergies, gastroesophageal reflux disease (GERD), radiation treatment for head and neck tumors, autoimmune problems (rheumatoid arthritis, lupus), and parasitic infections (trichinosis and leishmaniasis). Often, however, there is more than one cause. For example, one individual may have a viral respiratory infection that causes laryngitis, be a smoker, use improper vocal technique for singing, and have GERD. As with other vocal problems, therefore, it is important to identify all contributing causes for the problem. The most common cause of laryngitis in infants and children is acute infection, whereas noninfectious, chronic causes are more typical in adults (Koufman, 1996). GERD is probably the most common cause of laryngitis (55%), followed by smoking (25%). Table 3.1 lists some of the common causes of laryngitis.

The vocal symptoms of laryngitis are mild or moderate hoarseness and breathiness, low pitch, edema, and erythema (redness). Pain may be present, and swallowing may be difficult. Typically, the infection is self-limiting, lasting up to 10 days (Koufman, 1996). However, it is not uncommon for the dysphonia to last for a much longer period of time, as the individual uses incorrect compensatory strategies to produce voice during the time of the inflammation. In other words, the person begins some bad vocal habits during the period of inflammation, and these cause the dysphonia to be maintained.

Acute Laryngitis

Acute laryngitis can be infective or noninfective. The infective type is typically viral and occurs with an infection of the upper respiratory system (Mathieson, 2001). Acute noninfective laryngitis can be caused by trauma to the larynx, such as a severe episode of vocal abuse or exposure to an environmental irritant.

While most types of acute laryngeal infections are relatively benign, some are more dangerous, particularly in the case of infants and very young children. Acute laryngotracheitis, commonly called croup, is a disease affecting very young children. The subglottal area tends to be most

TABLE 3.1 SOME CAUSES OF LARYNGITIS

Acute	Chronic
Vocal abuse	Vocal abuse
Environmental irritant	Laryngopharyngeal reflux
Laryngotracheitis	Smoking and alcohol
Supraglottitis	Autoimmune diseases
Influenza	Allergies

severely affected, and the child develops the characteristic "barky" cough, as well as hoarseness and inspiratory stridor. The disease can be life threatening if the airway is severely obstructed. Another serious form of laryngitis is acute supraglottitis (epiglottitis). Both adults and children can be affected, although the disease is more common in young children. This disease is associated with severe throat pain, difficulty swallowing, and drooling. A high fever develops, and the epiglottis and aryepiglottic folds are very swollen and red. It is important to get medical help as soon as possible, because the airway can become seriously obstructed in a matter of hours, resulting in death.

Chronic Laryngitis

Chronic laryngitis is a condition in which the mucous membrane of the vocal folds is inflamed and swollen. This problem is often seen in individuals who smoke, use alcohol, and overuse their voices. Such individuals may also cough habitually, clear their throats to try to get rid of the irritation, suffer from gastric reflux, and have seasonal or chronic allergies. The laryngoscopic signs of chronic laryngitis include thick, sticky mucus and thickening of the epithelium. The soft pliant epithelium may become replaced by fibrosis, and when this happens, the initial pain of the irritation dissipates. The person's voice is typically low pitched, hoarse, and breathy, and may be weak in volume.

Treatment of chronic laryngitis is directed at eliminating the cause of the problem, such as smoking or another form of phonotrauma. A systematic program of vocal hygiene may be very helpful (see Chapter 7). Other contributing causes, including GERD or allergies, should be identified and treated as appropriate.

The most common cause of chronic laryngitis is reflux. Because the pharynx is situated directly behind the larynx, the highly acidic gastric contents can easily reach the posterior portions of the larynx, washing the delicate and sensitive tissues in acid and resulting in inflammation. Many patients seen in otolaryngology practices suffer from reflux. These individuals typically do not suffer from the usual complaints of heartburn. Rather, their symptoms include hoarseness, particularly in the morning; sensation of a lump in the throat; dysphagia; chronic throat clearing and chronic cough; aspiration; and laryngospasm (Sataloff, Castell, Katz, & Sataloff, 2006). The term *laryngopharyngeal reflux* (LPR) is therefore used to distinguish these clients from those with gastroesophageal reflux.

There are several important differences between GERD and LPR. First, people with GERD typically have esophagitis (inflammation of the esophagus), whereas those with LPR do not. Second, most individuals with GERD have lower esophageal sphincter problems, but those with LPR seem to have upper esophageal sphincter problems. Third, most GERD patients have nocturnal symptoms, when they are lying down and asleep, whereas LPR patients have more symptoms during the daytime, while in the upright position. In addition, LPR can lead to abnormal laryngeal muscle tension, and is often associated with edema, nodules, granulomas, laryngospasm, and esophageal cancer (Sataloff et al., 2006). Individuals who smoke are more susceptible to gastric reflux, because smoking lowers the pressure in the lower esophageal sphincter, between the esophagus and stomach, making it easier for the stomach contents to escape into the esophagus. Laryngoscopic findings include reddened arytenoids, vocal fold edema, and redness and swelling of the entire larynx, particularly the posterior portion, as well as dilation of small blood vessels and leukoplakia (white, thickened patches on the mucous membrane).

Contributors to reflux include fats, alcohol, chocolate, and spicy foods, as well as eating just before going to bed. The listed foods, in addition to tobacco smoke, affect the pressure of the lower esophageal sphincter, making it easier for stomach contents to escape. Eating late at night and then lying down to sleep means that gravity is unable to help keep the contents in the stomach. Clients are encouraged to avoid caffeine and acidic foods such as tomatoes and citrus, as well as alcohol and tobacco, and to not eat for 2–3 hours before bedtime. Also, clients may be advised to raise the head of the bed so that gravity can help to keep the stomach contents down. Vigorous exercise can also result in reflux, particularly when done shortly after eating (Rothstein, 1998, cited in Mathieson, 2001).

The occurrence of LPR is also widespread in infants and children. However, the diagnosis may be more difficult to establish in young children because they experience physiological regurgitation due to their immature digestive systems, making it difficult to differentiate between normal and pathological reflux.

In recent years, it has become easier to diagnose LPR using double-probe 24-hour ambulatory pH monitoring. In this procedure one probe is placed slightly above the lower esophageal sphincter, and another is placed above the upper esophageal sphincter, behind the laryngeal inlet. These probes accurately sample the acid levels at these two places for a 24-hour period, and levels are then compared with normal values. Treatment is aimed at reducing acid levels by changing eating habits and through use of antireflux medications such as omeprazole, famotidine, and cimetidine. These medications either reduce or completely block acid production in the stomach.

Immunocompromise and Autoimmune Diseases

People with compromised immune systems due to AIDS or other systemic diseases are susceptible to various types of opportunistic infections, many of which affect the larynx and vocal folds. These include oral, pharyngeal, laryngeal, and esophageal candidiasis, which causes dysphagia and pain on swallowing; cutaneous, oral, pharyngeal, and laryngeal lesions such as Kaposi's sarcoma, which is a type of malignancy; and chronic cough and dyspnea due to repeated infections of the pulmonary system (Gray & Rutka, 1988).

Autoimmune diseases are caused by the body's aberrant response to its own cells. Of the several autoimmune diseases that affect the larynx, the best known is myasthenia gravis (see Chapter 5 for a detailed discussion of myasthenia gravis). Another autoimmune disease, systemic lupus erythematosus, affects primarily young women and is characterized by ulcers and perforations in the face, oral mucosa, nasal septum, and upper respiratory tract (Mathieson, 2001). Approximately one third of individuals with this disease have been reported to show laryngeal involvement including inflammation, infection, subglottic stenosis resulting from granulomatous inflammation, and epiglottitis (Teitel, Mackenzie, Stern, & Paget, 1992).

Rheumatoid arthritis is a relatively common autoimmune disease that can affect the joints of the larynx. Rheumatoid arthritis is an inflammatory autoimmune disorder that disrupts the normal structure and function of synovial joints, including the cricoarytenoid and cricothyroid joints (Koufman, 1996; Stemple, Glaze, & Klaben, 2000). The disease typically goes through acute and chronic phases. In the acute phase, the vocal folds are inflamed, and the arytenoid cartilages look swollen and bright red (Buckmire, 2001; Stemple et al., 2000). Pain is common during this stage of the disease. As the disease progresses and becomes chronic, the articular surfaces of the joints (the locations where the joints articulate) are destroyed, and the joint space becomes filled in with vascular, fibrous, and fatty tissue (Buckmire, 2001). The arytenoid mucosa look rough and thickened, but pain is not usual at this stage. The soft tissues surrounding the joint may also exhibit rheumatoid signs, including rheumatoid nodules. Rheumatoid laryngeal nodules are not uniform, but may appear as white submucosal nodules, polypoid lesions, or ill-defined masses deep within the vocal folds (Buckmire, 2001; Koufman, 1996).

Not all individuals with rheumatoid arthritis will exhibit laryngeal involvement. Koufman (1996) reported that, when examined postmortem, up to 87% of patients with rheumatoid arthritis had cricoarytenoid joint changes; however, only 17%–33% of such patients had clinical signs of laryngeal involvement, including posterior laryngeal inflammation and decreased arytenoid mobility. The symptoms of cricoarytenoid joint fixation are hoarseness, a laryngeal fullness feeling, and pain associated with inflammation of the joint. In more severe cases the joint may be completely fixed (ankylosed) and may imitate the appearance of vocal fold paralysis.

Rheumatoid arthritis is usually treated with drugs or surgery. The most common types of medications are anti-inflammatories and corticosteroids. If the individual's airway is compromised, an arytenoidectomy may be done. This procedure involves removing the arytenoid cartilage on the affected side and suturing the vocal fold in an appropriate position. Although the airway is improved with this treatment, the client's voice may be breathy. In addition, if rheumatoid nodules are removed from the vocal fold, scarring may occur, resulting in persistent hoarseness.

Paradoxical Vocal Fold Motion

Paradoxical vocal fold motion (PVFM) is also referred to by various authors as paradoxical vocal fold disorder, irritable larynx syndrome, paradoxical vocal cord movement, vocal cord dysfunction, and episodic paroxysmal laryngospasm. PVFM is a respiratory rather than a phonatory disorder, characterized by inappropriate vocal fold adduction during the inhalation phase of breathing. Stridor and dyspnea (difficulty breathing) result, with individuals reporting a feeling of tightness in the laryngeal area and a choking sensation. Depending on the cause, the airway obstruction may be intermittent or continuous, mild or severe (Koufman, 1996).

Causes of PVFM include gastroesophageal reflux disease (GERD), respiratory-type laryngeal dystonia, laryngeal dysfunction associated with asthma, and brainstem abnormalities resulting from congenital causes or from stroke and head trauma (Koufman, 1996). The most common cause of PVFM is reflux, because the highly acidic gastric fluids irritate the sensitive laryngeal tissues to the point of triggering an attack. The second most common cause is psychogenic, occurring primarily in teenagers (Koufman, 1996). In this group, the attacks come and go very suddenly, and the individuals appear to be unconcerned about the problem. Reportedly, in these cases it can be easy to either precipitate or ameliorate an attack, which would not be the case when the attack is caused by nonpsychogenic triggers. Typically, the person's history in these cases will indicate some kind of underlying problem, such as stress, family problems, and so on, and the attacks will occur at stressful times. However, it is important to keep in mind that psychogenic factors can coexist with physical or physiological factors, and that other triggers such as reflux may also contribute to the problem.

Other causes of PVFM include upper airway sensitivity to various substances, either internal, such as acid reflux or upper airway secretions, or external, such as gases from a chemical lab or factory, smoke, fumes such as sulfur dioxide, cleaning agents, mist, dust, and airborne pollutants (Andrianopoulos, Gallivan, & Gallivan, 2000; Mathers-Schmidt, 2001; Sandage, 2006). It has been hypothesized that these types of irritants trigger vocal fold closure as a protective response. In addition to these triggers, Morrison, Rammage, and Emami (1999) reported that half of their patients with irritable larynx syndrome were able to relate the onset of symptoms to viral illness, including upper respiratory infection, herpes infections, viral meningitis, Lyme disease, and Epstein-Barr infections. Morris (2006) noted that vocal cord dysfunction is characterized by laryngeal hyperresponsiveness resulting from inflammation and altered autonomic balance. A summary of the causes of PVFM appears in Table 3.2.

The major symptoms of PVFM are those indicating that the airway is obstructed—that is, stridor and dyspnea. Stridor is typically heard when the individual breathes in, differentiating this disorder from asthma, in which stridor usually occurs on exhalation. However, it is not uncommon for the exhalation phase to be affected as well, because once the laryngospasm has begun during inspiration, the hyperadduction of the vocal folds may carry over for a brief interval into the exhalation phase (Andrianopoulos et al., 2000).

Some sufferers report a feeling of panic that they are suffocating to death, and others have a warning that an attack is about to occur, such as the sensation of a lump in the throat or a sharp taste, followed by a sharp pain and

TABLE 3.2 SOME PROPOSED CAUSES OF PARADOXICAL VOCAL FOLD MOTION

Gastroesophageal reflux disease (GERD)

Laryngeal dystonia

Asthma

Brainstem abnormalities

Upper airway sensitivity

Viral illness

Exercise

Psychogenic

an uncontrollable cough, and then the attack. Other symptoms that have been reported are a feeling of dizziness or lightheadedness, numbness or tingling of digits or around the mouth area resulting from hyperventilation, wheezing, chest tightness, and shortness of breath (Deem & Miller, 2000; Morris, 2006). It is common for clients to report numerous visits to the emergency department or hospitalizations for their symptoms, and many have been prescribed asthma medications, to no avail. Vocal symptoms are often present, particularly during an attack, and can include hoarseness, breathiness, and even aphonia.

In addition to respiratory testing, a laryngoscopic test using nasoendoscopy is critical. The client is asked to perform various tasks requiring vocal fold adduction and abduction under different circumstances, such as during quiet breathing, phonating, sniffing, coughing, and singing. The diagnosis of PVFM is considered when the vocal folds adduct during inspiration and/or when the vocal folds are spasmodically unable to abduct during exhalation (Koufman, 1996). However, individuals whose PVFM is related to GERD may not demonstrate these laryngeal findings, but instead show features of reflux (Koufman, 1996). The characteristic vocal fold configuration typically seen in PVFM is a small diamond-shaped chink at the posterior glottis during inhalation, rather than a complete opening of the glottis. The anterior two thirds of the vocal folds are adducted during inspiration, leaving the posterior diamond-shaped glottal gap. The absence of this posterior glottal chink does not mean that PVFM can be ruled out as the diagnosis (Andrianopoulos et al., 2000). When present, this posterior chink may occur during both inhalation and exhalation. Further, the false vocal folds may also adduct (Mathers-Schmidt, 2001). Even when the person is not showing overt signs of the disorder, the true vocal folds may be adducting during respiration (K. B. Newman, Mason, & Schmaling, 1995; Powell et al., 2000).

In addition to pulmonary and laryngoscopic assessment, it is also important to take a detailed history from the individual. Many people report that their symptoms have a very abrupt beginning and ending. Adults are often aware of factors that trigger an attack, such as exercise, laughing, very hot or cold air, dust, or fumes (Mathers-Schmidt, 2001). Children and adolescents tend to experience the attacks during physical activity and during stressful times in their lives. During the evaluation the examiner should ask questions such as whether the breathing difficulty occurs on inhalation and/or exhalation; whether stridor occurs when the individual is experiencing symptoms; whether bronchodilators are effective; and whether the individual has the sensation of choking or suffocation (Cookman, n.d.). The clinician and client should also discuss laryngeal symptoms, including any type of dysphonia; laryngeal sensations, such as a tight feeling in the throat; other bodily sensations, such as numbness or tingling in the hands or feet or around the mouth with attacks (Cookman, n.d.); and triggers for the attacks, such as GERD, nasal symptoms (e.g., congestion or postnasal drip), and exercise.

Individuals with PVFM may require treatment for an acute attack and/or long-term therapy. Clinical management can include pharmacological therapy, respiratory procedures, behavioral voice therapy, or any combination of these. For an acute attack, the sufferer may benefit from inhaling a mixture, known as heliox, that consists of 70% helium and 30% oxygen (Deem & Miller, 2000; Mathers-Schmidt, 2001). Heliox reduces the density of the inhaled air, making it easier for the client to breathe. In turn, this lessens the individual's anxiety and helps prevent the attack from becoming worse (Morris, 2006). Sometimes, the administration of continuous positive air pressure (CPAP) may be helpful. This procedure involves wearing a mask connected via a tube to a small instrument that delivers a steady stream of slightly pressurized air. The high pressure overcomes obstruction in the airway and stimulates normal breathing. This procedure has been reported to increase lung volume and slow the exhalation, which results in a more widely open glottis, and thus decreases the airway obstruction (Goldman & Muers, 1991, cited in Mathers-Schmidt, 2001). Some clients may need medications for conditions that contribute to the PVFM. For instance, when the trigger for the attacks is GERD or other irritants, the appropriate drugs should be administered to eliminate the precipitating condition. Also, some individuals with PVFM feel anxiety due to the feeling of suffocation. Because anxiety may worsen the symptoms, antianxiety medications may be useful in these cases. As a last resort, an individual may have to be tracheotomized if he or she does not respond to other types of therapies.

Behavioral therapy is often the treatment of choice and has been shown to be very helpful for individuals to manage the symptoms of the disorder. See Chapter 7 for a discussion of behavioral treatment strategies.

Chronic Cough

Chronic cough can be a symptom of or a coexisting factor with many different voice disorders. Chronic cough is differentiated from acute cough, which typically results from a viral infection and resolves within 3 weeks. According to Sandage (2006), cough becomes chronic if it lasts for more than 3 weeks, is not related to an active infection or disease process, and presents as a dry cough without productive mucus. Other authors have classified cough into acute, subacute, and chronic. Acute cough lasts for less than 3 weeks, subacute cough lasts from 3 to 8 weeks, and chronic cough persists for more than 8 weeks (Holmes & Fadden, 2004).

The primary causes of chronic cough, other than viral infection, are postnasal drip, asthma, and GERD. Chronic cough also can be a side effect of a class of medications known as angiotensin-converting enzyme (ACE) inhibitors or can occur secondary to chronic bronchitis from exposure to cigarette smoke or other irritants (Holmes & Fadden, 2004). As with many other disorders, chronic cough may result from more than one cause. Also, in some instances, chronic cough may be psychogenic. There are some differences between psychogenic and nonpsychogenic cough. First, the individual with a psychogenic cough does not cough while asleep and is therefore not awakened by the cough. Second, the person with psychogenic cough does not cough while engaged in distracting activities.

Although a cough might seem to be a simple problem, complications are common, including fatigue, change in social function, and trouble sleeping. Other side effects include disruption of normal activity including work, worry about serious medical illness, frequent retching, exhaustion, embarrassment, self-consciousness, and difficulty speaking on the phone (Vertigan, Theodoros, Gibson, & Winkworth, 2006). There can be physical manifestations as well, such as increased pressure on lumbar disks, laryngeal trauma, and urinary incontinence (Vertigan et al., 2006).

Medical management should include assessment and treatment for pulmonary disease, asthma, postnasal drip syndrome/rhinitis, gastroesophageal reflux, or laryngopharyngeal reflux. Endoscopic assessment of the larynx should be completed on all clients to rule out laryngeal pathology that may be triggering the cough, such as contact ulcer. It is also important to identify any triggers for the cough and to refer the person to an allergist if it seems that allergies may be triggering the cough response.

Behavioral treatment for chronic cough may be appropriate after all potential medical causes have been ruled out or treated. Treatment techniques are designed to teach clients to voluntarily suppress the cough (Vertigan et al., 2006). Strategies that focus on relaxation of extrinsic and intrinsic laryngeal muscles have been found to be helpful, as well as those aimed at reducing the force of vocal fold closure, such as yawn–sigh and easy-onset techniques (see Chapter 7). Teaching the client to perform exercises that are incompatible with the cough behavior is another effective strategy, such as pursing the lips and blowing slowly through them (Gallena, 2007). Abdominal breathing techniques may also be effective in reducing the cough behavior. A program of vocal hygiene and vocal education is often necessary to assist the client to make optimal use of the laryngeal mechanism (see Chapter 7).

Although PVFM and chronic cough are often discussed as though they are separate entities, recent research has suggested that there may be links between them. One possibility is that the cough may actually be a symptom of PVFM. Murry, Tabaee, and Aviv (2004) noted that chronic cough has been described to occur in as many as 80% of patients with PVFM. Another suggestion is that coughing might help open the vocal folds during an attack of PVFM (Blager, 2000). Alternatively, the PVFM may be the cause of the cough ("Chronic Cough," n.d.). Furthermore, Vertigan et al. (2006) suggested that chronic cough and PVFM may fall at opposite ends of a continuum with pure cough on one end, pure PVFM at the other end, and a combination of features in the middle.

Chapter 4
Nonorganic Disorders

Nonorganic voice disorders, which are also called psychogenic or functional voice disorders, are those disorders that result either in part or wholly from stress, anxiety, personality issues, mental illness, sexual issues, and/or gender identity problems. As with other types of voice problems, nonorganic disorders may have coexisting factors, such as vocal abuse, gastroesophageal reflux disease (GERD), allergies, and so forth. In fact, it may be difficult in some cases to determine whether the psychological factors have caused the problem, are maintaining the problem, or are the result of a pre-existing voice problem.

In most nonorganic disorders the larynx itself is normal but vocal function is impaired (Baker, 2002; Seifert & Kollbrunner, 2005). The impairment is often caused by excessive hyperadduction of extrinsic and intrinsic laryngeal muscles resulting from stress. Stress is typically associated with increased muscle tension throughout the body, and particularly in the head and neck region. When the larynx and vocal folds are extremely tense and constricted, the entire larynx may be elevated in the neck, resulting in an abnormally high pitch. Stress can create other bodily changes that affect voice, such as increases in heart rate, decreases of vocal tract secretions, and increases in gastric acid production. Decreased vocal tract secretions can result in dehydrated vocal folds, causing the voice to be produced with excessive effort and tension. Increased acid production can result in GERD, a factor that can create or worsen vocal problems (see Chapters 2 and 3).

Physical health also influences emotional status and vocal function. Individuals with severe or life-threatening conditions such as cancer or degenerative neurological diseases must cope with stresses related to fear, anxiety about the future, pain, loss of income, loss of control, expenses related to treatment, and other serious issues. In addition, family roles and relationships may be changed, adding yet another source of stress. All psychological, social, and emotional issues are critically important to address during the diagnostic and treatment process for a voice disorder.

Personality factors may also be associated with voice disorders. For instance, people with vocal nodules tend to be sociable, dominant, and aggressive; gravitate toward leadership roles; and like to be at the center of attention in social situations. This outgoing personality type could lead to prolonged talking at high volumes, with hyperadduction of the vocal folds and hard glottal attacks.

Symptoms and Features of Nonorganic Disorders

Vocal symptoms of nonorganic disorders are extremely varied and may include any one or a combination of features such as breathiness, hoarseness, harshness, strain, and pitch and loudness problems. Problems can range from slight to severe or, in extreme cases, total aphonia. While there are many different symptoms and characteristics of nonorganic voice problems, there are also certain features that many of these problems have in common (see Table 4.1). First, the symptoms are inconsistent with the clinical examination; the vocal folds may either behave normally, or the voice may be much worse than the vocal fold appearance would suggest. Second, the presentation is not consistent; that is, the individual's voice may vary depending on the context, subject matter, and mood. Third, the history and presentation of symptoms may be inconsistent with any known condition. Fourth, the disorder may be episodic, with periods of normal voice interspersed with periods of abnormal voice. Fifth, using various therapeutic approaches, a normal voice may be produced. Sixth, individuals with nonorganic voice disorders may be anxious and lack self-assertiveness (Seifert & Kollbrunner, 2005). Finally, these individuals often have a history of related stressful events or prolonged stress (Mathieson, 2001).

It is important to keep in mind that neurological and psychogenic voice problems can coexist, and differentiating the two components may be difficult. Other factors, such as GERD, allergies, and vocal abuse, may further complicate the diagnostic picture.

Conversion Disorders

Conversion disorders reflect a physical or physiological manifestation of a psychological problem. Sometimes a person suppresses a conflict or emotional problem rather than dealing with it consciously, and the problem manifests itself in a physical symptom, often related symbolically to the problem. A person whose conflict has to do with some aspect of communication—be it in a personal relationship or in an educational or professional context—may present with conversion aphonia or dysphonia. Conversion disorders reflect the loss of voluntary control over striated muscle

TABLE 4.1   COMMON FEATURES OF NONORGANIC VOICE DISORDERS

Normal larynx with good vocal fold closure on cough

Voice may vary depending on context

Vocal presentation may be incompatible with any known condition

Disorder may be episodic with periods of normal voice

Normal voice may be produced with trial therapy

Individual may be anxious and lack self-assertiveness

Disorder can be linked in time to a stressful event

or the sensory systems as a reflection of stress or psychological conflict (Caputo-Rosen & Sataloff, 1998). In the case of the laryngeal system, the vocal folds are capable of movement, and the person is able to cough, laugh, and perform other reflexive laryngeal behaviors. However, during volitional phonation, the vocal folds either do not move at all, resulting in aphonia, or do not move adequately, resulting in various degrees of dysphonia such as hoarseness and breathiness. Typically, the larynx is kept in a state of excessive tension. Sometimes the client presents with a falsetto voice and may also experience pitch breaks (Baker, 2002). In a true conversion disorder, the symptoms conform to the individual's idea of the disability, so there may be anomalies (Mathieson, 2001). For example, most people are not aware that the vocal folds are used for vegetative purposes such as coughing and laughing, so someone with a true conversion aphonia will likely cough and laugh normally. (Table 4.2 lists common features of conversion aphonia.)

When an individual with conversion disorder attempts phonation, the vocal folds may open rather than close, or they may partially close into a loose approximation (Deem & Miller, 2000). The person is not pretending or malingering—the vocal problem is real. The trick is to help the individual overcome both the vocal and psychological problem without making the person feel that he or she is crazy or that the problem is "all in the head." However, as Caputo-Rosen and Sataloff (1998) pointed out, sometimes what may seem to be a conversion disorder turns out to be the

TABLE 4.2 FEATURES OF CONVERSION APHONIA

Normal structure and function of the larynx

Loss of control over motor and/or sensory system

Problem related to anxiety, stress, and/or conflict

Disorder is symbolically linked to the conflict

Disorder allows person to avoid a situation

first signs of a neurological disease, so a thorough evaluation is of utmost importance to rule out central nervous system or peripheral nervous system dysfunction. It is not unusual for neurological and psychological diseases to occur together, a condition known as *somatic compliance*.

Onset of the psychogenic voice problem may be sudden, or the individual may experience recurring episodes of aphonia. Many clients associate the onset with some kind of illness or infection. In fact, many people with psychogenic voice disorders report some kind of chronic health problems related to the respiratory tract (e.g., asthma, bronchitis, frequent upper respiratory infections) and/or digestive tract (Andersson & Schalen, 1998; Baker, 2002).

The number of people with true conversion aphonia is small. According to Mathieson (2001), most cases of nonorganic aphonia are stress related. People with stress-related aphonia are typically women, who present as tense, anxious, and upset, often crying or being close to tears as they describe their situations.

Treatment of conversion aphonia focuses on both restoring normal vocalization and resolving, as far as possible, the psychological issues that created the voice problem. Numerous reports in the literature document that behavioral voice treatment is often relatively quick and effective. Counseling techniques are important to help the individual uncover and deal with the conflict in more open and productive ways. This necessitates an in-depth interview, with a detailed history relating to all aspects of the individual's life. To probe the person's feelings, the clinician must be both sensitive and matter-of-fact in his or her interactions with the client. Sometimes, as a client talks about concerns and conflicts in his or her life, the voice spontaneously reverts to a more normal vocal quality. For some individuals, however, direct voice therapy is needed to reestablish an improved voice. One technique is to manipulate the individual's larynx to release the muscular tension (see Chapter 7). Another strategy is to help the person to shape a reflexive vocalization such as a cough or a laugh into voluntary phonation.

When working directly with the voice, it is important to keep in mind that the person's voice may go through many stages before normal quality is achieved, and that some of the stages may actually sound perceptually worse than the previous dysphonia (Baker, 2002).

Transsexual / Transgender Voice

A transsexual person is one whose sexual and gender identity is fundamentally in conflict with his or her biological gender, and has been since early childhood, a condition termed *gender dysphoria*. This condition occurs in both males and females, although it seems to be more common in males. Usually, the individual feels strong discomfort with his or her biological identity, and the corresponding roles, expectations, and attitudes that society expects to go along with male and female genders. Typically, the person lives for years in accordance with the societal rules for his or her biological gender, enduring deep psychological distress because of the conflict. Eventually, the person may seek help and may decide to undergo surgical procedures for changing sexual identity. The process of changing one's sex is a long and challenging one, involving stages of counseling and psychotherapy, living as a person of the target sex, enduring the surgery itself, and going through the process of becoming accepted as a person of the target sex. The treatment of the transsexual client has been described as a process of phases through which one travels to get to the other gender side (Gold, 1999).

Surgery for changing one's sex is not done lightly. In fact, there are guidelines that have been widely adopted (called the Harry Benjamin guidelines for Standards of Care), which contain built-in time restraints and safeguards for the potential transsexual client. These include intensive counseling before being treated with hormones, in conjunction with at least a year of living as the target gender, prior to surgery (Gold, 1999).

Most individuals who go through with the surgery are male-to-female transsexuals. Often, the surgery is extremely successful in terms of visual appearance, with the help of appropriate hormone treatment, breast augmentation, electrolysis, facial plastic surgery, and so on. However, male-to-female transsexuals are often left with a voice that is male, at odds with the new appearance. The person's pitch levels, intonation patterns, voice quality, and overall communicative characteristics remain in the masculine domain. This is troublesome to many people who have undergone the surgery, and society does penalize people whose voices do not match their gender and build. Many transsexuals turn to voice therapists for help in achieving a more feminine voice.

Raising the pitch is typically the most important vocal goal in treatment of transsexuals. Research has established a cutoff fundamental frequency (F0) of 150–160 Hz, below which speakers are perceived as male and above which speakers are perceived as female (Gelfer & Schofield, 2000; Wolfe, Ratusnik, Smith, & Northrop, 1990). The goal of intervention is to achieve a mean F0 level as close as possible to that of female speakers, which is around 190–220 Hz. Various surgical and behavioral procedures have been used in an attempt to raise pitch.

Surgical techniques can be an important means of increasing the femininity of the individual's voice, because even when behavioral voice therapy is effective, uncontrolled vegetative vocalizations (e.g., laughing, coughing, yawning) may still occur in the male register (Gross, 1999). The goal of surgery is to increase vocal fold tension and thus raise the fundamental frequency. The most commonly used procedure to achieve this objective is cricothyroid approximation. In this technique the posterior cricoid is tilted backward and the anterior thyroid is tilted forward. The vocal folds are thus elongated and stretched, resulting in a higher pitch. The procedure is performed under local anesthetic, so the individual can phonate and the optimal pitch level can be determined. There are some disadvantages to this technique, however. First, this procedure is not always successful, due to various anatomical reasons. Second, the resulting pitch level may be in the falsetto range (Rammage, Morrison, & Nichol, 2001), which can sound unnatural. Third, the effect may not be permanent.

Another procedure, called laser-assisted anterior commissure placation, is used to create an anterior web. The effect is a shortened vibrating portion of the vocal folds, with a resulting higher pitch. The mucosal lining of the anterior quarter of the folds is vaporized with a CO_2 laser, and the denuded folds are sutured together (Rammage et al., 2001). Although this procedure does raise pitch, it can also generate breathiness or huskiness, and could decrease the individual's intensity level. In a similar technique, called endoscopic vocal fold shortening, the anterior portion of the folds is de-epithelialized and the corresponding tissue is sutured together. The vocal folds are thereby shortened, and their vibrating mass is reduced. Gross (1999) presented results demonstrating not only an average increase of 9.2 semitones in F0, but also a reduction in range in the lower frequencies.

In addition to raising pitch, many other aspects of communication need to be addressed in treating the male-to-female transsexual client. Features such as intonation, articulation, and nonverbal gestures should be part of a holistic and individualized treatment program. See Chapter 7 for a more detailed discussion of behavioral strategies.

Selective Mutism

Selective mutism, a rare disorder that typically manifests in early childhood, is believed to be strongly associated with anxiety and social phobia. This disorder used to be called "elective mutism," implying that the affected individual had a certain degree of control over the disorder, but the name has been changed to better reflect the underlying features. Specific criteria, listed in the *Diagnostic and Sta-*

tistical Manual of Mental Disorders–Fourth Edition–Text Revision (DSM-IV-TR; American Psychiatric Association, 2000), must be met for a diagnosis of selective mutism to be made. The primary factor in this disorder is that the child is able to speak, able to understand, and able to express him- or herself, but does so only in certain situations and not in others. The following are essential features of the disorder, as listed in the DSM-IV-TR:

1. The individual consistently fails to speak in specific social situations in which there is an expectation for speaking.
2. The disturbance interferes with educational or occupational achievement or with social communication.
3. The duration of the disturbance is at least 1 month and is not limited to the first month of school.
4. The failure to speak is not due to a lack of knowledge of, or comfort with, the spoken language required in the social situation.
5. The disturbance is not better accounted for by some other communication disorder such as stuttering, and does not occur exclusively during the course of pervasive developmental disorder, schizophrenia, or other psychotic disorder.

Typically, the child with selective mutism is excessively shy and withdraws in social situations. The degree of severity varies across clients in terms of both communication impairment and setting. Clients also vary in terms of associated or coexisting language disorders. Many children with this disorder do not have associated expressive or receptive language problems. However, reports vary in terms of the percentage of children who do have other concurrent problems. Atoynatan (1986) reported that approximately 20% of children with selective mutism may also have other speech or articulation difficulties. Baltaxe (1994) reported a considerably higher number of coexisting language problems in 24 children with selective mutism: 75% had articulation problems, 86% failed auditory processing measures,

60% demonstrated receptive language problems, and 75% showed expressive language deficits.

A thorough case history is important to obtain information regarding the behaviors that the child exhibits and the settings in which he or she does and does not communicate. The evaluator should gather information from the child's parents, siblings, other relations, teachers, friends, and so on. The clinician should also obtain data on whether the child achieved speech and language milestones at appropriate ages, as well as probe the child's current receptive and expressive language abilities in terms of phonology, morphology, syntax, semantics, and pragmatics. Family history and environmental influences should also be analyzed to determine whether there are any predisposing factors such as mental health issues, whether more than one language is spoken in the house, and whether the child has adequate language stimulation. It is also important to evaluate whether the child has other problems that may contribute to the disorder, such as neurological problems or hearing impairment.

Behavioral treatment based on operant conditioning is often the strategy of choice for treating the child with selective mutism. Two specific techniques include stimulus fading and shaping. Stimulus fading is a technique in which the child is gradually trained to develop new communication behaviors in small steps. For example, at a beginning level the child and his or her parent with whom the child communicates verbally interact in the clinical setting. As the child becomes more comfortable, another person is introduced into the setting and the child is reinforced for communicating with the other person. Another way of using stimulus fading is to have the child initially communicate nonverbally using gestures or writing, and then to increase the demand for verbal speech. Giddan, Ross, Sechler, and Becker (1997) provided a systematic procedure for progressing from nonverbal to verbal communication. In this program the child initially uses nonverbal gestures to communicate. Once the child is comfortable using nonverbal means, he or she progresses to verbal communication, moving from less propositional speech such as tape recordings of oral reading of stories, to propositional speech using soft whispering to various people, to loud whispering. Once the child is whispering consistently, the clinician helps the child to establish nonmeaningful vocalizations such as animal sounds and coughing. From this point the child is then required to use a soft voice in all school situations, and then a full voice both at school and in everyday situations.

Another behavioral technique is shaping, also called successive approximation. Shaping is used to elicit a target behavior in small steps by reinforcing those behaviors that come progressively closer to the final goal. To achieve this, the clinician breaks down the long-term goal into smaller steps or subtasks and reinforces the child for achieving each short-term goal. In the case of a child with selective mutism, any movement of the mouth that the child makes spontaneously can be rewarded initially, then only those that approximate speech movements. Once the child is accustomed to making the oral-motor movements without verbalization, the clinician introduces whispering and talking. In combination with such behavioral techniques, it is important that the family, teachers, and other important figures in the child's life should be involved as well. For example, parents may videotape a child reading aloud or talking in the home environment, and this tape can serve as a basis for discussion and reinforcement of the child's progress, both with the child and with his or her teachers.

Muscle Tension Dysphonia

Emotional difficulties, stress, and anxiety can result in physiological aberrations in vocal function. One such category of problems has been identified as muscle tension dysphonia (MTD), also known as muscle misuse dysphonia (MMD).

The primary characteristic of MTD is hyperfunction of the intrinsic and extrinsic laryngeal muscles, as well as muscles in other areas such as the face, neck, and shoulders (Roy, Ford, & Bless, 1996). The tension is noticeable in the client's neck, jaw, shoulders, and throat, and the individual often reports pain in these areas, as well as excessive vocal effort and vocal fatigue (Stemple, Glaze, & Klaben, 2000). Often, the person's larynx is elevated in the neck. Symptoms of MTD range from mild to severe, with varying vocal qualities including breathiness, hoarseness, and strain. The symptoms tend to worsen with increased voice use (Ford & Bless, 1996).

Dysphonias caused by muscle tension and misuse are probably the most common cause of nonorganic and non-neurological voice problems (Angsuwarangsee & Morrison, 2002). In all probability MTDs are caused by many interacting factors, including heavy voice usage and psychological and/or personality factors that induce tension and poor vocal technique. In some cases the problem may arise when the speaker habituates a pattern of straining to produce voice following an upper respiratory tract infection. In other cases the individual may exert excessive vocal force to compensate for an underlying problem such as vocal fold paralysis or bowed vocal folds.

Laryngoscopically, there are certain patterns of laryngeal positioning that are suggestive of MTD. For instance, the vocal folds may be hyperadducted laterally at the level of the vocal folds or at supraglottal sites, or both. In supraglottal compression the false vocal folds adduct during phonation. This type of false vocal fold closure is also called ventricular phonation. In some cases the true vocal folds may also be adducted, while in others the true vocal folds remain open. The resulting voice quality depends on whether the true vocal folds are open or closed in conjunction with the false folds (Rammage et al., 2001). When the true vocal folds are closed, the individual's voice is high pitched and "squeaky," whereas loosely opened true folds result in breathiness or a "tense whisper." Deem and Miller (2000) suggest that in supraglottal compression, the false folds may actually rest on the true folds, which adds mass to the true folds and hampers their vibration. Thus, the resulting voice is low pitched and hoarse, and pitch range is often decreased as well. When the true vocal folds are compressed but the false vocal folds are appropriately open, the resulting voice is harsh and tense, and the individual typically uses hard glottal attacks for voicing onsets. This type of compression is usually due primarily to poor vocal technique.

Another pattern of vocal fold closure seen via laryngoscopy is called anteroposterior supraglottal compression. In this pattern the front and back edges of the vocal folds are squeezed toward each other, with the arytenoid cartilages in the back of the larynx pulled forward toward the base of the epiglottis in the anterior portion of the larynx. This pattern is typically seen in conjunction with an extremely low-pitched speaking voice, which has given rise to the name "Bogart–Bacall syndrome" (Koufman & Blalock, 1988). Both actors, Humphry Bogart and Lauren Bacall, were instantly recognizable by the low-pitched, gravelly sound of their voices. This type of MTD is characterized by extreme effort to produce voice at the low pitch ranges and by rapid vocal fatigue. In addition, the finding of poor breath support is very common (Blalock, 1992). Most individuals with this syndrome tend to speak with an inadequate air supply (sometimes called "residual air"), which increases the degree of muscle tension needed to produce the desired pitch and volume of the voice (Koufman & Blalock, 1988).

A videolaryngoscopic evaluation is important to determine the presence and degree of lateral and/or anteroposterior tightening. In addition, the clinician can manually palpate the laryngeal area to determine areas of tension and/or pain. This technique is known as manual circumlaryngeal assessment. The clinician applies pressure in certain areas, such as over the major horns of the hyoid bone, over the superior horns of the thyroid cartilage, and into the suprahyoid muscles (Ford & Bless, 1996). MTD is suspected when the pressure causes discomfort or pain for the client. The discomfort tends to be unilateral but may radiate to one or both ears. The clinician also moves the individual's larynx gently from side to side and notes the ease (or lack of ease) with which it moves. Difficulty in this lateral motion indicates generalized tension in the suprahyoid muscles. In addition, the clinician can feel the thyrohyoid space between the posterior borders of the hyoid bone to the thyroid notch. A restricted thyrohyoid space suggests that the excessive muscular tension is causing the larynx to be carried abnormally high in the neck.

During manual examination of the larynx, the clinician can attempt manipulations of the larynx that may improve the speaker's voice, indicating that muscle tension may be the primary factor in the dysphonia. For instance, while the person phonates, the clinician can put gentle downward pressure on the larynx, or compress the larynx by putting pressure on the hyoid bone, or both. If these movements result in improved voice (by briefly interrupting the excessive tension and stabilizing the larynx), then MTD is likely to be the cause of the problem (Ford & Bless, 1996). As well as being diagnostic, these types of applications of manual pressure can be used as part of treatment (see Chapter 7).

Treatment typically focuses on relaxation methods. A general progressive relaxation approach may help the client to identify specific sites in the body where excessive muscular tension occurs and learn to contrast these with states of relaxation. The individual then learns to consciously and systematically control his or her bodily tension. More direct techniques of reducing laryngeal tension may also be valuable. For instance, massage is helpful: If a muscle is too tense, it is overly contracted and shortened; massaging the muscle helps to lengthen and relax it (Verdolini, 1998). A technique that uses such massage is called circumlaryngeal manual massage or laryngeal manipulation (see Chapter 7).

Puberphonia

Puberphonia, also called mutational falsetto, occurs in postadolescent males. During puberty, the male's larynx and vocal folds show a dramatic growth spurt, resulting in the longer, thicker vocal folds of the adult male, with the associated lowered pitch. Occasionally, despite this laryngeal growth, a male's pitch level will not lower, often due to psychological reasons, such as resistance to the responsibilities of adulthood, embarrassment at the pitch changes and voice arrests that occur during the change, or desire to identify with the female sex. The abnormal voice may also be the result of the individual's attempt to stabilize the unsteady pitch and quality of the changing vocal mechanism. Instead of the normal lower pitched adult voice, the individual attempts to maintain the higher pitch of his pre-puberty years, a feat that requires a great deal of laryngeal muscular force and tension to achieve. In this type of phonation, vocal fold vibration is extremely rapid and the folds do not close completely during vibration. Thus, the voice is not only abnormally high pitched, but also breathy and weak. The individual's larynx may be hypertonic, and the cartilaginous glottis may be closed too tightly so that only the membranous portion of the vocal folds is able to vibrate (Rammage et al., 2001). This would also contribute to the excessively high pitch, because the effective vibrational length of the vocal folds is decreased. In addition, the entire larynx is elevated due to excessive contraction of the suprahyoid muscles, contributing to the overall impression of abnormally high-pitched and weak voice. In addition to these vocal factors, the person may carry his tongue in an abnormally high position, which further changes vocal tract resonance (Stemple et al., 2000). With an abnormally high-pitched voice, males are commonly mistaken for females over the phone and are stereotyped as being passive and immature. However, it is important to rule out other causes of the high pitch, such as endocrine problems, hearing loss, or neurological problems.

With structural or other possible causes ruled out, behavioral voice therapy is the treatment of choice for mutational falsetto. Laryngeal massage may be effective in producing a lower pitch (see Chapter 7). Other techniques for eliciting a more normal pitch level include having the individual cough or laugh. These vegetative vocalizations are likely to occur at a more normal pitch level, and can then be shaped into meaningful utterances. It has been well documented that many clients respond favorably and quickly to these types of interventions, and a normal adult male voice is often achieved within the first or second therapy session. The challenge becomes to help the person to accept his new voice, which may both sound and feel uncomfortable at first. However, as the individual experiences more favorable social attention, he typically becomes more confident with the new voice and begins to habituate it in everyday situations.

Chapter 5
Neurogenic Disorders

Neurogenic voice disorders result from strokes; progressive degenerative diseases such as Parkinson's disease, multiple sclerosis, and amyotrophic lateral sclerosis; traumatic brain injury; and congenital malformations of the brain. Neurogenic voice disorders are often referred to as dysarthrias. *Dysarthria* is an umbrella term for a group of speech production disorders caused by various neurological problems in which the primary problem is weakness, paralysis, or incoordination of the speech musculature. Dysarthrias can affect any or all of the systems involved in speech production, including respiration, phonation, and articulation. Dysarthrias have been classified on the basis of site of brain damage and the resulting type of movement disorder. Darley, Aronson, and Brown, in 1969, wrote a seminal article categorizing the dysarthrias, based on the authors' experience with hundreds of patients with speech and voice disorders at the Mayo Clinic. Their widely used classification scheme has six categories of motor speech disorders: flaccid, spastic, ataxic, hypokinetic, hyperkinetic, and mixed. When the dysarthria primarily affects the phonatory system, the disorder is referred to as a dysphonia. Flaccid dysphonia, spastic dysphonia, and hypokinetic dysphonia are examples of dysphonic disorders. Table 5.1 lists the dysarthria (aka dysphonia) classification, with associated site of damage and resulting voice symptoms.

Flaccid Dysphonia

Flaccid dysphonia results from damage to the lower motor neuron of the brain, consisting of the spinal and cranial

TABLE 5.1 CLASSIFICATION SYSTEM FOR DYSARTHRIAS

Type of dysarthria	Site of brain damage	Primary voice symptoms
Flaccid	Lower motor neuron	Breathy, weak
Spastic	Upper motor neuron	Low pitch, strain-strangle
Ataxic	Cerebellum	Prosodic abnormality, scanning speech
Hypokinetic	Basal ganglia- Substantia nigra	Monotone, weak
Hyperkinetic	Basal ganglia	
Chorea		Prosodic abnormality
Dystonia		Effortful, strain-strangle
Mixed	Various	Depends on affected areas

Note. Adapted from "Differential Diagnostic Patterns of Dysarthria," by F. L. Darley, A. E. Aronson, and J. R. Brown, 1969, *Journal of Speech and Hearing Research, 12,* pp. 246–256.

nerves, and the myoneural junction between the nerve ending and the muscle that it supplies. Examples of disorders resulting in flaccid dysphonia are vocal fold paralysis and myasthenia gravis.

Vocal Fold Paralysis

Vocal fold paralysis (VFP), the most common disorder associated with flaccid dysphonia, accounts for 10% of all laryngeal problems (Andrews, 1995). It may occur at any time period in a person's life, from infancy to old age. In infants, VFP may result from birth trauma or may be secondary to congenital heart problems, surgery, or other medical procedures (Andrews, 1995). In adults, the causes of VFP are numerous, including viral infections, stroke, progressive neurological diseases (e.g., multiple sclerosis), head trauma, infectious diseases, cancer that invades the nerve, and thyroid surgery. In fact, damage to the recurrent laryngeal nerve during thyroid or heart surgery is the most common cause of VFP (Mathieson, 2001; Rammage, Morrison, & Nichol, 2001). Sometimes, however, the cause of the paralysis is unknown, in which case the disorder is called idiopathic vocal fold paralysis.

The paralysis may be unilateral or bilateral, and the fold(s) may be fixed in either adducted or abducted positions. The symptoms, therefore, depend on the position of the paralyzed fold(s) and can include not only problems in vocal production, but problems in breathing, swallowing, and coughing as well. If only one fold is paralyzed close to the midline, the individual's voice may be slightly breathy, with decreased loudness. Diplophonia may be present. With the fold paralyzed further from the midline, the breathiness and weakness will be more pronounced. If both folds are paralyzed, the symptoms will be even more severe, with possible aphonia rather than breathiness. Folds that are paralyzed in the closed position result in symptoms associated with airway obstruction rather than vocal problems.

One closed fold results in a fairly normal voice, with mild stridor during exertion. If both folds are fixed in an adducted position, the individual must be tracheotomized or intubated immediately, or death will result.

Another factor that affects the resulting voice is the location of the damage. The larynx is innervated by the vagus nerve, cranial nerve X. Three branches of the vagus are critical in speech production: The pharyngeal branch supplies motor impulses to the soft palate, the superior laryngeal branch innervates the cricothyroid muscle, and the recurrent laryngeal branch supplies the other four intrinsic laryngeal muscles (lateral cricoarytenoid, posterior cricoarytenoid, interarytenoid, and vocalis). If the nerve is damaged before it begins to branch, then all three branches will be affected. This means that all structures supplied by these nerves will be paralyzed, including the soft palate and all the intrinsic laryngeal muscles. The speaker, in this case, would have problems with hypernasality, breathiness, and pitch regulation. If only the pharyngeal branch is affected, hypernasality would be present, but the laryngeal muscles would be intact, so phonation would not be impacted. If only the superior laryngeal nerve is affected, the result would be problems with pitch, but vocal fold abduction and adduction would be unaffected. With only the recurrent laryngeal nerve affected, abduction and adduction would be disordered, but pitch control would be intact.

When both folds are paralyzed, problems can occur not only with phonation but also with respiration and/or swallowing. If both folds are paralyzed in the closed position, immediate surgery is required to establish an adequate airway. In this case, an arytenoid cartilage may be removed completely or may be sutured in a more appropriate position to create an airway. Both folds paralyzed in the open position results not only in aphonia but also in swallowing problems such as aspiration of foods. In fact, individuals with bilateral paralysis may need to be fed via a nasogastric tube, to prevent aspiration (Stemple, Glaze, & Klaben, 2000).

It is not unusual for the paralysis to resolve spontaneously within 6 months to 1 year of onset. Because of this possibility, surgery is usually not performed right away. Many surgeons require clients to wait 9 to 12 months, unless an individual has serious problems with swallowing and aspiration.

There are two commonly used major surgical approaches to vocal fold paralysis: injection and thyroplasty. An approach that has been in use for many years for unilateral paralysis is the injection into the paralyzed fold of a substance such as Teflon, Gelfoam paste, fat, or bovine collagen. The rationale is that this will increase the bulk of the fold and make it easier for the unaffected fold to cross over the midline and make contact with the paralyzed fold, resulting in improved closure for vibration. This procedure often produces a clearer and stronger voice quality. Although the synthetic substance Teflon has been used for many years, it has disadvantages. The Teflon may migrate from its original site of injection within the fold to a different location, or it may cause an allergic reaction that creates inflammation and the formation of granuloma tissue. Also, the procedure is not reversible. Fat and collagen tend to produce fewer allergic reactions; however, these substances are more easily absorbed into the host tissue, so the beneficial effect may not last very long. Because injection of fat involves harvesting fat from the person's abdomen through liposuction or an open incision (Rosen & Soose, 2006), the individual has to undergo additional procedures. For temporary improvement (i.e., while waiting to see if the paralysis will resolve spontaneously), a substance called Gelfoam is often used. Gelfoam is a gelatin powder that turns into a paste when mixed with saline. The paste is injected into the paralyzed fold. The Gelfoam is absorbed into the body after around 4–12 weeks (Rosen & Soose, 2006).

The other surgical option is a procedure called thyroplasty. In this procedure, the surgeon cuts a small window into the thyroid cartilage and places a piece of a synthetic substance called Silastic behind the paralyzed vocal fold.

This has the effect of pushing the fold toward the midline, thus allowing the intact fold to make easier contact, while not interfering with the medial edges of the fold involved in vibration. This procedure has advantages over injection, as there is no associated inflammation. Additionally, better vocal fold closure is often achieved, and the procedure is reversible. Further, the procedure is done under local anesthetic, so the individual assists in the creation of an improved voice by phonating at various times during the process. Thus, the degree of vocal fold tension that creates the best voice quality can be determined in conjunction with the speaker and the speech–language pathologist. In order for the person to achieve his or her best possible voice, the vocal fold must be positioned appropriately in three planes: medial–lateral, superior–inferior, and anterior–posterior (Rosen & Soose, 2006). To achieve this goal, an additional procedure called an arytenoid adduction may be done. In this technique, the muscular process of the arytenoid of the affected fold is sutured to another point in the larynx, and the tension of the suture is adjusted to stretch and medialize the fold (Rammage et al., 2001). Thus, the positioning of the folds can be adjusted in various ways to create the best possible voice for the individual.

Behavioral voice techniques are sometimes successful in improving vocal fold closure. The individual is taught to close the folds forcefully using a pushing technique (see Chapter 7) so that the intact fold can cross over the midline and contact the paralyzed fold. Another important goal of voice therapy is to prevent the client from developing maladaptive compensatory behaviors in an effort to increase loudness. The most common techniques are those that focus on teaching good vocal hygiene, including modification of voice use, and on changing the environment in various ways to facilitate less abusive vocal usage (Rosen & Soose, 2006). Another technique is resonant voice therapy or similar techniques (see Chapter 7) that aim to lessen the muscle tension dysphonia that often accompanies the speaker's attempts to compensate for the problem.

Myasthenia Gravis

Myasthenia gravis (MG) is another example of a nervous system disorder that results in flaccid dysphonia. The outstanding characteristic of this disease is that the individual's movements in the affected structure(s) become progressively weaker with repetition in an extremely short period of time (i.e., seconds or minutes). Thus, if the person's larynx is involved, he or she may start out phonating relatively normally, but within a minute or so, the voice becomes progressively weaker, breathier, and more hypernasal, to the point where the individual cannot sustain the phonation. There are often other symptoms typical of flaccid muscle movement, such as difficulty chewing and swallowing, difficulty smiling, a weak and ineffective cough, and dulled facial expression.

Myasthenia gravis is an autoimmune disorder that affects the myoneural junction, the location where the nerve meets up with the muscle. The problem is that the person's antibodies destroy the acetylcholine receptors at the myoneural junction, so that nerve impulses are prevented from getting into the muscle and stimulating it to contract. The head and neck muscles tend to be involved at the early stages of the disease; in fact, the structures that are important for speech are often the first to be affected. The disease can progress to affect other structures. MG is most common in young and middle-aged women, but it also occurs in men. Sometimes the disorder is localized to the larynx, in which case it is called myasthenia laryngis.

Diagnosis of MG is based on the way that the muscles fatigue and recover rapidly. A drug, such as Tensilon or neostigmine, can be injected while the individual is using the affected body part. If the drug improves the function within a very short period of time, MG is suspected. In addition to drugs, tests to assess muscle function more directly, such as electromyography, can be used for diagnosis.

The choice of treatment depends on the severity of the disease, as well as the person's age and general condition.

The most popular treatment for MG is the administration of cholinesterase inhibitors, such as Mestinon and Prostigmin. These chemicals prevent the acetylcholine from being reabsorbed by the presynaptic neuron too soon, so the neurotransmitter is available in the myoneural junction for a longer period of time. Removal of the thymus gland is also recommended for most individuals, because of the strong correlation between thymus function and MG. Corticosteroids such as prednisone often provide relief of symptoms, as do immunosuppressant drugs such as azathioprine and cyclosporine. Finally, a procedure called plasmaphoresis, or plasma exchange, is used when an individual's symptoms suddenly become markedly worse or when he or she has not responded to other types of treatment. In this procedure the individual's plasma is filtered and the antibodies that are causing the problem are removed.

Spastic Dysphonia

Spastic dysphonia results from damage to the corticobulbar tracts of the upper motor neuron. The corticobulbar tracts are the nerve pathways that run from the motor areas of the cortex on either side of the brain to the medulla, controlling movement on the same side of the body. Speech is affected when the damage is bilateral, but few, if any, effects occur from unilateral damage. This is because the nerve supply from the corticobulbar pathway to the vagus nerve is bilateral. Thus, if only one side of the corticobulbar tract is affected, the vagus nerve still receives innervation from the other side. There are many causes of bilateral damage, including stroke, trauma, tumors, infection, and progressive diseases such as multiple sclerosis and amyotrophic lateral sclerosis.

Damage to the corticobulbar tract causes spasticity. A spastic structure is one in which the muscle tone is excessive, so the structure is rigid and difficult to move. It may also be weak or even paralyzed. In the case of spastic dysphonia, the range of motion of the vocal fold is limited because it is difficult to move the spastic folds. The resulting symptoms are typically a very low-pitched voice with a strong strain-strangle component. In addition, the ventricular folds may adduct, resulting in a harsh voice quality (Andrews, 1995). A characteristic symptom is uncontrollable laughter or crying, without the associated emotions. Swallowing is always affected (Mathieson, 2001), and hypernasality is common because of lack of coordination of the velum with the other articulators. The speaker may also have difficulty coordinating breathing and phonation, which can result in very short phrases of one or two words before he or she needs to take another breath.

Treatment is usually pharmacological, with the aim of reducing the spasticity. Antispasmodics such as Dantrium and Lioresal are often prescribed. Valium is a muscle relaxant that may be used. Behavioral voice treatment is not typically indicated because of the underlying neurological problem.

Cerebellar (Ataxic) Dysphonia

The cerebellum functions to coordinate movement in terms of speed, direction, timing, range, and force, and is also involved in the regulation of muscle tone; thus, damage to this part of the brain results in movements that are uncoordinated and jerky. Damage may occur from stroke, tumors, cerebral palsy, infectious diseases, and so on. Genetic syndromes with ataxia as one of the characteristics are not uncommon causes.

For the speech and voice production muscles to be affected, the damage to the cerebellum must be widespread and severe. When this is the case, the individual's voice is often abnormally slow and lacks the normal prosody of speech, a condition sometimes called "scanning speech." The person loses the ability to coordinate the fine vocal fold movements needed to regulate the pitch and loudness changes that contribute to the rhythm and stress of the language. When a word or syllable is stressed, the pitch is raised slightly, volume is increased, and the syllable is briefly extended in duration. Without the ability to make these fine distinctions, the prosody and rhythm of the language are lost. The person's speech may also be slurred, with monotone pitch and loudness, hoarseness, and tremor. The client often shows an intention tremor, that is, a tremor that occurs with purposeful movement but disappears at rest.

There is no specific treatment that targets vocal symptoms of ataxic dysphonia. Surgical or pharmacological treatments for the underlying cause or for associated symptoms may be provided as appropriate.

Hypokinetic Dysphonia

Hypokinesia refers to movements that are abnormally reduced in amplitude. Hypokinetic dysphonia is associated with Parkinson's disease (PD). PD is a neurological syndrome that typically results from the loss of the neurotransmitter dopamine, manufactured in the substantia nigra of the basal ganglia. The basal ganglia is the name for a collection of subcortical grey matter that are involved in the inhibition of excessive movement generated by the motor cortex. PD can result from degenerative, vascular, or inflammatory changes in the basal ganglia. It can also follow from encephalitis or result from the use of drugs called neuroleptics, which are used to treat certain mental illnesses. The most common cause of Parkinson's disease, however, is idiopathic, with no specific precipitating cause. Approximately .5 million people in the United States suffer from PD (Merati et al., 2005).

Dopamine acts to refine and smooth voluntary movements. Loss of dopamine results in an excess of muscle tone, or rigidity, which is one of the major symptoms of Parkinson's disease. The muscular rigidity typically results in a blank look on the individual's face, resulting from the inability to move the facial muscles. This is termed a "masked facies." Another symptom is tremor, which usually occurs when the affected structure is at rest. When the tremor affects the person's hands, there is often a characteristic rolling movement of the fingers, called a "pill-rolling" movement. Another consequence of loss of dopamine is a condition called bradykinesia, which is a slowness of movement that impairs both walking and writing. In terms of the laryngeal system, the rigidity of the vocal folds makes it difficult to achieve normal vibration. The person's voice typically is characterized by very weak intensity, monopitch, monoloudness, and varying degrees of hoarseness and breathiness. Vocal symptoms can be the first obvious sign of the neurological problem, or can develop later as the disease progresses. The disease is most common in individuals in the middle years (age 50 and over), but it can also occur in younger adults.

Because PD is progressive, symptoms are often described in stages. One staging system, the Hoehn and Yahr staging of Parkinson's disease (Hoehn & Yahr, 1967), describes five levels of increasing severity. In Stage One, symptoms are unilateral and mild, with tremor only in one limb. Stage Two presents with bilateral symptoms, as well as disturbances in posture and gait. By Stage Three, bodily movements become significantly slower. Stage Four includes rigidity and bradykinesia. At this stage the individual is no longer able to live independently, and by Stage Five he or she cannot stand or walk, and requires constant care. Along with the movement disorder that affects speech and swallowing, other problems in PD include intellectual deterioration and depression.

The primary treatment of PD is pharmacological, and most people are treated with the drug levodopa (L-dopa) either by itself or in combination with other drugs. Levodopa is a substance that is converted into dopamine in the brain, thus replacing the dopamine that is lacking in the basal ganglia. This reduces the primary problems of rigidity and tremor. However, levodopa can have severe side effects such as involuntary tics (dyskinesia) and nausea. Therefore, the drug is often taken in combination with other drugs (e.g., carbidopa) to reduce the side effects. The levodopa–carbidopa combination is highly effective, but a disadvantage is that doses usually have to be increased over time. Additionally, an "on–off" pattern can occur in which the drug does not work for unpredictable periods of time (Henkel, 1998).

Because drugs used to treat PD have potentially severe side effects and are not completely effective for many individuals, there is growing interest in the use of surgical techniques. Several types of surgical procedures, such as pallidotomy and thalamotomy, have been developed to treat the rigidity, bradykinesia, and tremors. In a pallidotomy, a small portion of the globus pallidus (part of the basal ganglia) is destroyed by a tiny electric probe. While this procedure can markedly reduce the tremors and rigidity, it can also leave the individual with impaired speech. Similarly, a thalamotomy is a procedure in which specific areas of the thalamus, a subcortical structure, are destroyed in order to reduce tremors. Another recently developed surgical procedure is the implantation of fetal cells into the brain. Called fetal cell transplantation, the aim of this procedure is to increase the production of dopamine. Research on a small number of patients has shown that while the procedure has beneficial effects on the motor system in general, the effects on voice production are not pronounced (Farrell, Theodoros, Ward, Hall, & Silburn, 2005).

Another recent development is the use of tremor control implants. Implant wires are surgically inserted into a brain area such as the thalamus, and a pulse generator is implanted in the person's chest. The device, when activated by the individual, transmits electrical impulses to the brain, which has the effect of blocking the tremors (Deem & Miller, 2001; Henkel, 1998).

In addition to pharmacological or surgical management, behavioral voice treatment can be beneficial. Traditional "pushing" techniques (see Chapter 7) that help the client increase the forcefulness of vocal fold closure during vibration can increase his or her loudness level. In the 1990s, Ramig and her colleagues developed a systematic protocol that uses this principle of increased forcefulness to help the individual achieve and maintain a louder voice (Ramig, Countryman, Hoehn, O'Brien, & Thompson, 1996; Ramig, Countryman, Horii, & Thompson, 1995). Called the Lee Silverman Voice Treatment (LSVT), this program is an intensive treatment given in 16 sessions in 1 month. The program is designed to help the individual to use a higher level of effort to overcome the rigidity and hypokinesia of the laryngeal system, and to make this new level habitual (see Chapter 7 for a detailed description). Research has shown this program to be highly effective in generating and maintaining higher levels of vocal volume as well as increased intelligibility.

Hyperkinetic Dysphonia

Hyperkinetic dysphonia refers to the presence of random, involuntary, uncontrollable movements that interfere with normal motor function. The movements may be choreic (i.e., quick and jerky) or dystonic (i.e., slow and sustained). The movements may occur in the limbs and/or the muscles of the face, jaw, tongue, and larynx. Hyperkinetic dysphonia, like hypokinetic dysphonia, results from damage to the basal ganglia, but to different parts of the structure than are involved in Parkinson's disease.

Chorea

The most common disease resulting in chorea is *Huntington's disease* (HD), a genetic disease caused by a problem with a specific gene protein on chromosome 4. In a way that is not yet understood, this problem results in damage to the basal ganglia and cerebral cortex. It is an autosomal dominant disorder, meaning that if one parent is affected, each of the offspring has a 50% probability of inheriting the disease. Typically, the disease manifests itself later in life, between ages 35 and 50 years. By this time it is likely that the person has had children, who in turn have a high probability of inheriting the disease. The number of individuals in the United States who either have the disease or are at risk for getting the disease is relatively high, around 250,000.

Huntington's disease is progressive and is characterized by a set of clinical features that include emotional, cognitive, and motor disturbances. Symptoms include chorea, clumsiness, slurred speech, depression, irritability, apathy, memory loss, and attention deficits. Swallowing is also affected, and death usually occurs 10–25 years after the initial diagnosis from choking, infection, or heart failure.

Voice and speech are commonly affected when laryngeal and articulatory muscles are involved. The individual's prosody is likely to be disrupted by erratic and unpredictable fluctuations in pitch, loudness, breathiness, and hoarseness. Likewise, articulation may be disrupted by random and uncontrollable movements of the tongue, lips, jaw, and velum. In addition, the individual may make facial grimaces, as well as sucking and lip-smacking movements (Rosenfield, 1991). Respiratory support for speech becomes impaired. Speech problems appear early in the disease and progressively worsen. The individual typically becomes unintelligible and may over time become completely nonverbal.

Because the genetic marker for HD has been identified, individuals who are affected or at risk can be tested for the defective gene. However, there is no specific treatment, and no cure has been found. Treatment is targeted to particular symptoms, such as drugs to treat the motor disturbances, antidepressants to treat the depression, antipsychotics, and mood stabilizers. As with PD, surgical techniques such as fetal tissue transplantation, pallidotomy, and thalamotomy may be attempted to alleviate the motor symptoms.

Currently, although research is underway, the disease is

incurable and the progression can not be stopped. However, the speech–language pathologist can play an important role in educating caregivers, family, and friends in how to communicate effectively with the affected individual. The clinician can also help the client to maximize his or her communication by increasing respiratory support for speech and improving phonatory function.

Chorea can also result from extended use of neuroleptic drugs used to treat certain mental illnesses, and the disease in this kind of situation is known as tardive dyskinesia.

Dystonia

The involuntary movements in dystonia are more sustained than those in chorea. They tend to build up gradually to a peak and then gradually subside. Similar to chorea, the movements are random and unpredictable, and they interfere with normal movement control. The dystonia may be generalized to the entire body, a condition called *dystonia musculorum deformans*, or may be limited to a specific part of the body or a specific structure, a condition known as *focal dystonia*. Spasms of the tongue, mouth, jaw, and pharyngeal muscles are known as *oromandibular dystonia* (Bloom & Ferrand, 1997). Focal dystonias are typically induced by a specific type of task or activity. Dystonia can be isolated, with no other neurological problems, or it can occur in conjunction with other problems such as tremors. As with chorea, neuroleptic drugs can cause the onset of dystonia, which is another form of tardive dyskinesia.

Voice symptoms in dystonic conditions may be characterized by changes in quality, pitch, and loudness; hypernasality; and stridor. Often, there are inappropriate intervals of silence and unpredictable stress patterns (Bloom & Ferrand, 1997). High levels of stress tend to increase the dystonic symptoms. The most common type of focal dystonia that a speech–language pathologist is likely to encounter is spasmodic dysphonia.

Spasmodic Dysphonia

Spasmodic dysphonia (SD) is a descriptive term that refers to a voice disorder characterized by spasms of either the adductor or abductor muscles. This disorder used to be considered psychogenic because one of its hallmarks is that it is highly resistant to behavioral voice therapy. Another reason is that it is induced by voluntary phonatory activity. Thus, when the person tries to talk normally, the problem manifests itself, but when the person uses the laryngeal muscles reflexively, such as for coughing, the muscle function is normal. Vocal function is also within normal range for phonatory activities such as singing, speaking at a higher than normal pitch, and whispering. In the past, individuals with this disorder were shunted from therapist to therapist, and often tried such methods as psychiatry, hypnosis, acupuncture, and others, to try to find some relief from this disabling problem. However, research conducted over the past two to three decades has demonstrated that most cases of SD are neurogenic in nature and are most likely due to a focal dystonia (e.g., Blitzer, Lovelace, Brin, Fahn, & Fink, 1985; Feldman, Nixon, Finitzo-Hieber, & Freeman, 1984).

Spasmodic dysphonia may be of the adductor, abductor, or mixed variety. Adductor SD is characterized by spasms of the adductor muscles (called laryngospasms) and is the most common form of the disorder. Depending on the severity of the disorder, the supraglottal structures and the pharyngeal muscles may adduct in addition to the true vocal folds. The spasms result in a voice quality that is strained-strangled, with an effortful, jerky tone that sounds like the person is straining to push out voice. Sudden voice arrests are common and can result in speech that sounds stuttered. In severe cases the individual may grimace or appear to be struggling to breathe with the effort. The increased effort needed to produce voice may be felt by the client in the articulators, as a sensation of being strangled, as a burning sensation in the throat, or as tightness across the chest and abdomen when speaking (Stewart, Brin, & Blitzer, 1997). The disorder can coexist with a tremor, which would give the voice, in addition to the other symptoms, a quavery, tremulous quality. Some speakers may strain so intensely to produce voice that they produce grunts, groans, and squeaks along with the voice. Onset of the disorder is typically in adulthood and is usually gradual, becoming progressively worse over some years. Clients often, but not always, report first noticing symptoms either coinciding with or immediately after a viral infection or some kind of unusual emotional stress. Symptoms usually worsen with stress, illness, or fatigue.

The abductor form of SD is much rarer than the adductor form. In this version, the abductor muscles spasm open involuntarily, giving the person's speech a breathy, jerky quality, but without the severe strain-strangle effect of the adductor type. The overall flow of speech is disrupted by intermittent periods of aphonia. As in adductor SD, a vocal tremor may be present in abductor SD. Often, the transitions from voiceless to voiced sounds are difficult and result in an effortful whisper or brief periods of silence between sounds. The mixed form of SD has both adductor and abductor characteristics.

Diagnosing SD is not straightforward, as there is no specific test for it. Rather, other conditions must be eliminated, and the diagnosis of SD must be based on behavioral and acoustic evidence. For example, it is important to distinguish between SD and muscular tension dysphonia (see Chapter 4). Stewart et al. (1997) noted that a diagnosis of SD is based on an individual's history, the perceptual symptoms (e.g., overall severity, roughness, breathiness, strained-strangled quality, abrupt voice initiation, voice arrest, aphonia, tremor, expiratory effort, related movements and grimaces), and the person's ability to modify the vocal characteristics during various phonatory and nonphonatory vocal activities. Laryngoscopic and acoustic evaluations are also important. During videonasoendoscopy the speaker's vocal folds are visualized during speech. This is essential, as the abnormal vocal fold movements are triggered by speech and tend to be within normal range during other types of vocal activities. Hyperadduction may involve only the true vocal folds or the true vocal folds plus false folds. In some cases the arytenoid cartilages may be pulled forward, and in extreme cases the arytenoid cartilages may touch the epiglottis (Stewart et al., 1997). In the case of abductor SD, the arytenoids can be seen to pull open during phonation.

Treatment for SD has undergone great changes over the past few decades. SD is typically highly resistant to traditional behavioral voice therapy, although mild cases sometimes do respond to techniques for lessening the force of vocal fold closure, such as yawn–sigh and gentle onset. Treatment aimed at alleviating the voice problem via psychological techniques has become less popular, because the cause of the disorder is now widely acknowledged as being neurological rather than psychological. Counseling techniques or psychological referrals are appropriate, however, if the client does have serious issues and concerns or needs help dealing with the effects of the disorder on his or her life.

Currently, surgical techniques are the most prevalent form of clinical management. In the late 1970s, a surgical technique called recurrent laryngeal nerve resection (RLN section) was introduced. This procedure aims to decrease the force of vocal fold vibration by severing the recurrent laryngeal nerve, thus inducing a unilateral vocal fold paralysis. However, over several years, long-term studies of the effectiveness of this technique showed that although the individual's voice was much improved after surgery, long-term results were poor, with many clients' voices becoming as bad as or worse than they had been before surgery (e.g., Aronson & DeSanto, 1983).

The current treatment of choice for spasmodic dysphonia is Botox injection (see Chapter 7). Botox is a neurotoxin that acts at the myoneural junction, preventing the transmission or release of acetylcholine and, therefore, resulting in a flaccid paralysis. The usual dosage for SD is around

2.5 Us (mouse units), injected either bilaterally or unilaterally, although the dosage is tailored to each individual's vocal profile and needs. The effects of the Botox last from 3 to 6 months. This procedure is highly effective for most affected individuals, resulting in a voice produced with considerably less effort. Typically, for the first few days after the injection, the person is somewhat breathy and may experience some difficulty in swallowing. These effects wear off, however, and the person is left with a usable voice.

Behavioral voice therapy has been shown to be valuable in conjunction with Botox injections. It is important for the client to learn principles of good voice usage and to eliminate vocally abusive behaviors. Therapy is also designed to decrease the amount of respiratory effort used to power voice production, thus decreasing hyperfunctional vocal fold closure. Voice therapy often prolongs the effective interval between Botox injections.

Organic Tremor

Organic tremor, also known as essential tremor or familial tremor, is considered by some voice researchers and clinicians to be a hyperkinetic dysarthria (e.g., Rammage et al., 2001), although no specific site of brain damage has been identified. It often occurs in conjunction with other dystonias, including SD. The tremor may be isolated to the laryngeal muscles or may be evident in other articulators, such as the lips, jaw, tongue, and soft palate, as well as in the head and hands. The rate of the tremor is around 4–8 Hz (Mathieson, 2001; Rammage et al., 2001; Stemple et al., 2000). If the tremor is familial, then it is inherited as an autosomal dominant gene. However, in many cases there is no obvious cause of the disorder, in which case it is called essential tremor rather than familial tremor (D. Newman & Ramadan, 1998).

The disease usually manifests itself during a person's middle to later years of life. The onset may be gradual or sudden (Andrews, 1995). This is not a progressive disorder, but the tremor is worsened by stress, fatigue, and excitement. The tremor tends to be more conspicuous when the person is using the affected structure for some kind of purposeful activity. This kind of tremor is known as kinetic tremor, or action-specific tremor. When the laryngeal muscles are affected, the vocal characteristics include rhythmic alterations of pitch and loudness that give the voice a quavery quality, as well as voice arrests. It is often possible to see the person's larynx moving vertically in concert with the voice arrests. Because voice arrests are common in SD as well, SD and organic tremor are sometimes confused and misdiagnosed. Essential tremor should be differentiated from tremors associated with other disorders such as Parkinson's disease, anxiety, and cerebellar disease. The tremor in these other disorders is usually slower than the rate of 4–8 Hz that is common in organic tremor.

Organic tremor is typically treated with drugs, such as beta blockers (e.g., propranolol) or anticonvulsants (e.g., primidone). These medications can reduce the amplitude of the tremors, but the problem is difficult to eliminate entirely (Deem & Miller, 2000). When the tremor is severe and resistant to medications, surgery may be considered. Surgical techniques are similar to those used to alleviate the tremors in Parkinson's disease, such as thalamotomy. The disadvantage of this procedure is that when done bilaterally, the risk of dysphonia is increased. A more recent technique that lessens the chances of side effects is called deep brain stimulation. A small hole is drilled into the individual's skull, allowing for an electrode to be positioned in a certain area of the thalamus. The electrode is connected to a lead that is implanted behind the ear and connected to a stimulator similar to a pacemaker, which is placed under the collarbone. The client regulates the stimulator by means of a magnet. The advantage of this procedure is that, rather than destroying brain cells, as is done in thalamotomy, the brain cells are temporarily disabled by the electrical stimulation generated by the electrodes.

Mixed Dysphonias

Damage to the brain can be widespread, affecting different areas that are involved in voice production. The resulting problems are characterized by different types and degrees of dysphonias, such as flaccid–spastic, spastic–cerebellar, and so on. Amyotrophic lateral sclerosis and multiple sclerosis are two degenerative neurological diseases that cause mixed dysphonias.

Amyotrophic Lateral Sclerosis

One of the best known mixed dysphonias is a flaccid–spastic dysphonia that results from *amyotrophic lateral sclerosis* (ALS), a progressive neurological disease also known as Lou Gehrig's disease or motor neurone disease. This disease strikes the lower and upper motor neurons, causing the nerves to degenerate with resulting scarring and hardening of the nervous tissue. As the nerves degenerate the person's voluntary muscles become progressively weaker, and eventually complete paralysis results.

The disease tends to strike individuals in the 40- to 70-year age range, although it can affect much younger individuals as well. The average time from diagnosis to death is around 3 years (Deem & Miller, 2000), with 10% of patients living more than 10 years with the disease. There are a few well-known cases of individuals who contracted the disease during young adulthood and lived for 30 or more years with the disease.

The cause of ALS is not known conclusively but may be linked to genetic, viral, autoimmune, and neurotoxic factors (Walling, 1999). Only 5% of cases have a clear genetic cause, in which case the disease is autosomal dominant. Theories attempting to explain causes of nongenetic cases are being explored. One such theory focuses on the role of the neurotransmitter glutamate. Too much of this neurotransmitter is toxic to nerve cells, and researchers in the

1990s (e.g., Lin et al., 1998) found that ALS patients had excessive amounts of glutamate in their nervous systems. This finding led to the development of a drug called riluzole, which inhibits the release of glutamate from neurons and has been shown to be fairly successful with some affected people in increasing survival rates.

Because ALS affects both lower and upper motor neurons, symptoms of both flaccid and spastic dysphonia occur. Symptoms of flaccid dysphonia include breathiness and weakness, while symptoms of spastic dysphonia include low pitch and a very tense and harsh quality. The speaker may also demonstrate tremor, unusual pitch patterns, limited pitch range, hypernasality, abnormally slow rate, and a hyperactive gag reflex (Andrews, 1995). The uncontrollable laughter and crying associated with spastic dysphonia may also be present. Because the individual is not able to swallow properly and clear mucus secretions, a wet, gurgly, hoarse voice quality may be present. Weakness and spasticity in the respiratory muscles also contribute to the speech production difficulties.

Diagnosis of ALS is made on the basis of laboratory tests, muscle and/or nerve biopsy, analysis of cerebrospinal fluid via a spinal tap, magnetic resonance imaging (MRI), electromyography (EMG), and nerve conduction velocity tests. There is no cure, and typically a combination of medications is used to control the symptoms of the disorder, as well as physical aids such as walkers, wheelchairs, and braces. Only one drug, riluzole, is currently on the market for ALS. Although the drug does not stop the progression of the disease, studies have shown that survival rates have increased for some patients taking the drug (Walling, 1999). Other drugs are used for different symptoms, such as baclofen, Valium, and Dantrium to relieve spasticity; antiinflammatory agents to relieve pain from muscle cramping; medications to reduce excess saliva production; and antidepressants to treat anxiety and depression, which commonly co-occur with ALS. In the later stages of the disease, the individual may become aphonic but may be able to use augmentative communication devices such as a communication board or some type of computerized system. Swallowing is typically a problem and requires appropriate treatment and compensatory strategies, such as the chin-tuck, which involves swallowing in a head-down position to minimize choking and coughing (Walling, 1999). As for other disorders that are far-reaching in their effects, treatment of the individual with ALS is best done in an interdisciplinary setting so that all areas of concern can be addressed. The speech–language pathologist plays a particularly important role by helping the person to maintain his or her most effective communication and swallowing.

Multiple Sclerosis

Another disease that results in a mixed dysphonia is multiple sclerosis (MS). This is a disease in which the myelin sheath that covers nerves in the central nervous system deteriorates, with subsequent scarring. The nerve axons themselves may be damaged or destroyed. The problem can occur anywhere within the central nervous system, including the cerebrum, spinal cord, cerebellum, brainstem, and spinal pathways (Andrews, 1995; Deem & Miller, 2000; Mathieson, 2001). The cause is thought to be an autoimmune disorder in which antibodies attack the myelin coating, resulting in subsequent inflammation and scarring. The progression of the disease is highly variable, both between and within individuals. Onset of the disease is typically between 20 and 40 years of age, with an average onset age of 30.

There are four different forms of the disease, each of which is characterized by a different pattern of acute flare-ups of symptoms (called relapses or exacerbations) and remissions. The most common form, called relapsing–remitting MS, is characterized by periods of remission interspersed with relapses. The individual may go for weeks or months without symptoms and then suffer a relapse lasting for some time. Secondary progressive MS is also characterized by relapses and remissions, but over time the relapses start to predominate, and the remissions become less frequent. The third type, called primary progressive MS, is characterized by a gradual but steady loss of function over a period of years, with no remissions in between. Finally, there is a progressive–relapsing form of the disease, in which there is steady worsening from the onset, in conjunction with acute relapses.

MS is characterized by muscular weakness and spasticity due to damage to the corticospinal pathways, ataxia resulting from cerebellar involvement, and various degrees of paresis and paralysis (Deem & Miller, 2000). However, because the demyelinization and inflammation can occur anywhere within the nervous system, individual symptoms and the course and progression of the disease vary greatly. Early symptoms may include impaired vision. As the disease progresses, the individual may develop other symptoms such as an intention tremor, dysphonia, and swallowing problems. Speech and swallowing disorders are fairly common. When speech and voice are affected, the resulting symptoms are characteristic of ataxic and/or spastic involvement, including reduced pitch and loudness ranges, changes in prosody, and a harsh voice quality (Deem & Miller, 2000). The individual may also demonstrate abnormal pitch and loudness control, hypernasality, impaired breath support, and the scanning speech (Andrews, 1995) that is characteristic of ataxic dysphonia.

Diagnosis of MS is based on various tests of nervous system structure and function. MRI is useful in visualizing the specific defects in the white matter and can also help to differentiate between old and new lesions (Ferrand, 2007). A lumbar puncture or spinal tap is done to extract cerebrospinal fluid and test it for the presence of inflammation. Tests of evoked potentials are used to measure how rapidly nerve impulses are conducted in the body. A slowing of nerve conduction rates suggests a problem with impulse transmission.

There is currently no cure for MS, but drugs are available that reduce the duration of relapses and actually slow the progression of the disability. Current forms of therapy are designed to change the response of the immune system. For example, corticosteroids can shorten the duration of the relapses. High doses of a type of drug called beta interferon may actually decrease the demyelinating activity. Interferons, which are proteins that occur naturally in the immune system, may help to reduce inflammation and regulate the abnormal immune response; therefore, beta interferon can be used in the relapsing–remitting form of the disease to reduce the frequency of relapses as well as physical disability. Some examples of beta interferons are Avonex, Betaseron, Rebif, and Copaxone. Other types of drugs are also becoming available. For example, taking a form of bovine myelin by mouth may stimulate remission of the disease (Fukaura et al., 1996). Amino acids such as glatiramer acetate can also reduce the frequency of relapses and the resulting physical disability (Edan & Coustans, 2000). Certain chemotherapeutic drugs are used to treat progressive forms of the disease, as well as cases of remitting–relapsing MS that are getting worse. Drugs to alleviate spastic muscles can be helpful, as in the other disorders that have spasticity as a feature. Two major antispasticity drugs are baclofen and Zanaflex. In addition to these types of medications, Botox can help to relieve spastic muscles. Shaking and tremors may be controlled with use of propranolol or similar drugs. Thalamic implants similar to those used in Parkinson's disease are currently being explored, although their use in MS is considered experimental. Fatigue is often a problem for patients with MS, and medications such as amantadine can work well. Antidepressants may be used to treat concurrent depression.

Behavioral voice treatment that focuses on respiration training and pushing exercises (much like behavioral treatment for Parkinson's disease) may be helpful in improving vocal fold closure and increasing loudness.

Chapter 6
Laryngectomy

The removal, either partial or complete, of a person's larynx is called *laryngectomy*, and the person who has been laryngectomized is known as a laryngectomee. This procedure is typically done when an individual has cancer of the larynx. Usually, the cancer affects the squamous epithelium of the vocal folds. This type of cancer, known as squamous carcinoma, makes up about 90% of head and neck cancers (Stemple, Glaze, & Klaben, 2000). Occasionally, the cancer will attack the cartilages rather than the epithelium, in which case it is called chondrocarcinoma and chondrosarcoma (Slavin, 1997). Based on data provided by the Surveillance Research Program of the American Cancer Society's Department of Epidemiology and Surveillance, Stemple et al. (2000) reported that cancer of the head and neck is the sixth most common form of cancer worldwide and that the larynx is the second most common site within the head and neck category. However, laryngeal cancers make up only 1% of all cancers. Stemple et al. (2000) also reported that most laryngeal cancers (56%) occur on the vocal folds, 31% occur supraglottally, and only around 1% occur subglottally.

Laryngeal cancer is more common in men than women, but in recent years the number of women developing the disease has increased substantially, probably due to the increased rate of smoking by women. Research has also shown that the incidence is higher for African Americans, due to factors including exposure to carcinogens in the home and/or workplace, and higher rates of tobacco and alcohol usage (N. Johnson, 2001). Mortality rates for African Americans are also higher than those for Caucasians, possibly because economically disadvantaged individuals wait longer to get medical attention and therefore seek medical care at more advanced stages of the disease (Slavin, 1997).

The survival rate for laryngeal cancer depends on how early the cancer is detected and treated. In very early stages, the prognosis is good, with a 5-year survival rate of 75% (Shah et al., 1997). When caught early, the cancer is slow growing and the laryngeal cartilages form a barrier that prevents the spread of the cancer from one side of the larynx to the other or from inferior to superior regions, or vice versa. The later the tumor is discovered and treated, however, the poorer the prognosis, because eventually the cancer will spread to the lymph nodes in the individual's neck, and from there, metastasized to other areas of the body.

Cancer Staging

Cancers are classified in a system called the TNM classification, developed by the American Joint Committee for Cancer Staging. In this system, T stands for tumor, N stands for nodes, and M stands for metastasis (American Joint Committee on Cancer, 2002). Categories are lettered and numbered according to the degree of spread of the tumor. A category of X indicates that information is not available, 0 indicates no involvement, and higher numbers indicate more involvement. Tis stands for carcinoma in situ, meaning that the cancer cells have not spread into the connective tissues of the larynx or pharynx but are confined to the epithelium.

In the T1 category, the tumor is limited to the vocal fold(s) and the vocal folds move normally. T1 is further categorized as T1a or T1b. In T1a the tumor is limited to one vocal fold, and in T1b the cancer is present on both vocal folds. A T2 tumor indicates that the cancer has spread into the supraglottis and/or subglottis, and/or there is limited movement of the vocal folds. T3 indicates one or more of the following: the tumor is limited to the larynx and there is no movement of the vocal folds; the tumor has invaded areas surrounding the glottis; and/or the thyroid cartilage has been invaded to a small degree by the cancer. The T4 category is also divided into T4a and T4b. T4a indicates that the tumor has invaded through the thyroid cartilage and/or extends to tissues beyond the larynx. In T4b the cancer has spread extensively so that it surrounds a carotid artery or is growing down into the front of the chest cavity.

Node categories range from 0 to 3. N0 indicates no evidence of any spread to the lymph nodes in the neck; N1 indicates one suspicious lymph node that is less than 3 cm (1.25 in.) in diameter; N2 indicates suspicious nodes on both sides of the neck, or more than one suspicious node at one side, or a large node on one side (up to 6 cm or 2.5 in.); and N3 refers to a suspicious node greater than 6 cm (2.5 in.) in diameter. Metastasis is either not present (0) or present (1).

Once the categories have been determined, the information is combined to assign an overall stage, ranging from 1 to IVC (see Table 6.1). A carcinoma in situ without any nodal involvement or metastasis (Tis, N0, M0) is classified as Stage 0. A small tumor confined to the vocal folds and having no lymphatic involvement or metastasis (T1, N0, M0) would be assigned to Stage I. Stage II involves a larger tumor but no spread to lymph nodes (T2, N0, M0); In Stage III there is some spread to the lymph nodes or the tumor is extensive (T1, 2, or 3; N1; M0, or T3, N0, M0). Stage IVA involves tumors of varying sizes but fairly extensive nodal involvement, or very extensive spread of the cancer with varying nodal involvement (T1, 2, or 3; N2; M0, or T4a; N0, 1, or 2; M0). Stage IVB involves very extensive tumor invasion with any amount of spread to lymph nodes, or any size tumor with extensive lymph node involvement (T4b, Any N, M0, or Any T, N3, M0). Finally, Stage IVC is applied to any situation in which metastasis has occurred (Any T, Any N, M1).

TABLE 6.1 TNM CLASSIFICATION SYSTEM FOR CANCER	
Stage	**Categories of involvement**
0	Tis, N0, M0
I	T1, N0, M0
II	T2, N0, M0
III	T1, 2, or 3; N1; M0
	T3, N0, M0
IVA	T1, 2, or 3; N2; M0
	T4a; N0, 1, or 2; M0
IVB	T4b, Any N, M0
	Any T, N3, M0
IVC	Any T, Any N, M1

The main factors for developing laryngeal cancer are smoking and drinking, although there are occasionally other causes, such as inhaled pollutants, radiation, and precancerous lesions of the larynx such as leukoplakia (Andrews, 1995). Mathieson (2002) reported that for individuals who smoked more than 35 cigarettes per day, the relative risk of developing cancer was 7 times greater than for nonsmokers; however, when the smoking was combined with drinking, the relative risk became 22 times as great.

Symptoms of laryngeal cancer vary, depending on the location and stage of the disease. A tumor on the vocal folds results in hoarseness, and possibly breathiness and low pitch. The greater the extent of the tumor, the more severe the dysphonia is likely to be. The individual may also experience stridor if the tumor obstructs the airway. Tumors above the vocal folds tend to produce dysphagia, pain that can be referred to the ear, and swelling of the neck. Tumors in the subglottal area may result in pain and difficulty breathing (Andrews, 1995). Other symptoms can include the sensation of a lump in the throat, persistent throat clearing and coughing, persistent sore throat, and unexplained weight loss (Stemple et al., 2000).

Nonsurgical Options

Treatment depends on the stage of the laryngeal cancer. For small tumors, radiation therapy and chemotherapy may be tried, or the growth may be removed microsurgically or with a CO_2 laser (Andrews, 1995). Radiation therapy has become quite popular in recent years as radiation treatments have become more refined, with less time involved and less destruction of healthy tissue. This type of treatment is able to preserve laryngeal function and is relatively cost-effective (Leeper, Parsa, Jamieson, & Heeneman, 2002). Cure rates have been reported to be similar for radiotherapy and other approaches, and consequently the preservation or restoration of voice has become an important factor in the type of treatment chosen (van der Torn, Verdonck-de Leeuw, Kuik, & Mahieu, 2002). In some cases, the patient is irradiated to decrease the size of the tumor, and then surgical treatment is performed. In other cases, the patient undergoes radiation therapy following surgery to make sure that all the cancerous growth has been removed. Following radiation treatment, permanent cure rates (after 3 years without recurrence) of 80%–90% have been reported, with fewer than 10% of patients needing a subsequent laryngectomy (Mathieson, 2001). However, it is important that patients be selected carefully for radiation therapy to be successful. The individual's tumor should be small and well differentiated, and should not extend to the subglottal area (Leeper et al., 2002).

Radiation therapy can have many side effects. Because radiation dries out salivary and mucous glands (Leeper et al., 2002; Orlikoff & Kraus, 1996), side effects of radiation can include dry mouth, as well as a drying out of the laryngeal mucosa that results in a kind of laryngitis called laryngitis sicca. Other potential side effects include severe edema, redness of the skin, sore throat, loss of taste, increased risk of dental caries (Andrews, 1995), and inflammation (Bertino, Bellomo, Ferrero, & Ferlito, 2001). Additional problems can include muscle atrophy, fibrosis of the soft tissues, keratosis, and dysphagia. However, Leeper et al. (2002) noted that, in spite of the side effects, most patients' voices improve with radiotherapy. The preserved voice, however, may still be dysphonic, with individuals reporting symptoms such as speaking with effort; reduced dynamic range; and lack of control over their voice quality, pitch, and loudness (Orlikoff & Kraus, 1996). In addition, the symptoms may be extremely variable and unpredictable, fluctuating over the course of treatment.

Even for advanced stage cancers, it is becoming more common to treat patients with nonsurgical methods such as radiation and/or chemotherapy in order to preserve the larynx and thus the voice (Orlikoff & Kraus, 1996). Recent reports indicate that simultaneous administration of radiation and chemotherapy has a cure rate comparable to that of surgery.

Surgical Options

As shown in Table 6.2, there are different surgical options depending on the site and extent of the tumor. Sometimes, removal of part or all of the larynx, as well as some or all of the lymph nodes in the neck, may be necessary. For a small, well-defined tumor on the anterior part of the vocal fold, a cordectomy (also called a lateral partial laryngectomy) may be done. This involves removing the diseased tissue together with a margin of healthy tissue around the tumor, either by cutting it away or by CO_2 laser. The surgeon cuts through the anterior part of the thyroid cartilage to reach the affected fold. Typically, the entire vocal fold is removed, and the resulting tissue may either heal spontaneously, or may be reconstructed by means of a mucosal flap taken from the false vocal folds (Bertino et al., 2001). In either

TABLE 6.2 SURGICAL OPTIONS DEPENDING ON EXTENT OF TUMOR

Cordectomy (lateral partial laryngectomy)

Partial laryngectomy (hemilaryngectomy, vertical partial laryngectomy)

Supraglottal laryngectomy

Near-total laryngectomy

Total laryngectomy

case the person is left with a workable, although dysphonic voice.

For more extensive cancers, there are various so-called conservation procedures that are designed to remove cancerous tissue while preserving as much of the healthy structure as possible. Again, the type of procedure that is chosen depends on the location and extent of the cancer (Doyle, 1997). For a tumor confined to one side of the larynx, a partial laryngectomy may be done (also called hemilaryngectomy or vertical partial laryngectomy). In these cases, the surgeon removes not only the vocal fold, but other structures on the affected side as well, including the thyroid and arytenoid cartilages and the false vocal folds. When healing takes place, a band of scar tissue forms, which acts almost like a surrogate vocal fold. Indeed, according to Mathieson (2001), the healthy fold may even be able to approximate the band of scar tissue, and the individual may be able to produce a reasonable voice, although there will be residual hoarseness and breathiness.

When the tumor occurs on the epiglottis and ventricular folds, without any spread to more inferior structures, a supraglottal laryngectomy may be performed. Structures excised in this procedure include the hyoid bone, epiglottis, ventricular folds, and some portion of the thyroid cartilage (Slavin, 1997). Even though the hyoid bone and thyroid cartilage may not be cancerous, they are removed to ensure that the cancer cannot spread. The vocal folds themselves are left intact, thus preserving the voice. Structures such as the epiglottis may be reconstructed, to help in swallowing and to prevent aspiration (Andrews, 1995).

When the cancerous lesion is extensive but confined to one side of the larynx, a near-total laryngectomy may be the most appropriate surgical procedure. The entire larynx is removed, but a narrow strip of tissue on the side opposite the tumor is allowed to remain, connecting the trachea and the pharynx. This piece of tissue is fashioned into a shunt. Because the entire larynx is removed, the individual needs a permanent tracheostoma through which to breathe, as in a total laryngectomy. When the stoma is occluded, pulmonary air from the trachea is directed through the shunt and into the pharynx. Thus, the person is able to produce esophageal voice.

When other methods of treatment have failed or when the cancer is extremely extensive, a total laryngectomy may be required. In this procedure the entire laryngeal framework is removed, including the hyoid bone and often the upper tracheal rings as well. The trachea is bent forward and sutured to a stoma created in the neck. Following surgery, breathing will take place only through the stoma, but the individual will be able to eat and drink normally. Air can get into and out of the lungs only through this new pathway, directly into and out of the trachea. Of course, without a larynx, the person is unable to produce voice in the normal way.

Problems Related to Surgery

Depending on the type of surgery performed, various problems occur both in communication and in physical and psychological aspects of functioning (see Table 6.3). Because total laryngectomy results in many physical changes, and not only the complete loss of normal voice production, the speech–language pathologist needs to be aware of these

TABLE 6.3 PROBLEMS RESULTING FROM TOTAL LARYNGECTOMY

Direct intake of air into trachea

Need to avoid water in stoma

Loss of ability to smell and taste

Difficulty adjusting to altered body image

Social and emotional difficulties

Loss of communication

problems and be able to either deal with them or refer the person to the appropriate professional. This is why a team approach to voice restoration and rehabilitation is crucial.

With the removal of the larynx, the individual breathes through the neck, which creates certain problems. Rather than inhaled air being warmed and humidified as it travels through the nose, taking air directly into the trachea means that the air is dryer and cooler. This tends to irritate the stoma and trachea, particularly at the beginning stages of recovery. The stoma becomes dry and crusty, and the laryngectomee needs to learn how to clean it. This could be a problem if the individual has dementia or has difficulty using his or her hands, as would be the case with arthritis. People in the client's environment also need to be aware of the problem and know how to help with proper hygiene.

Usually, individuals with stomas wear a stoma cover to prevent debris, dust, and particles from entering the stoma and the trachea. The cover also helps to warm the air within the space between it and the stoma, and helps during sleep by absorbing mucus. Also available are perforated stoma guards, worn between the stoma and the stoma cover, which prevent the cover from being sucked up against the stoma while breathing (Deem & Miller, 2000). There are also commercial systems available for filtering the air, called heat and moisture exchange systems. A piece of material is placed over the stoma; then as the individual inhales, the air is filtered and humidified by the natural moisture in the material created by the condensation from the exhalations, and is warmed by the material. This system is beneficial as it more closely resembles the warming and moistening of air that occurs in normal breathing. Thus, the buildup of mucus and the resulting irritation around the stoma and in the trachea are reduced. A "laryngectomy bib" serves a similar function, by absorbing mucus and warming inspired air. Other devices include foam squares, disposable filters that are held in place over the stoma by adhesive strips. These also warm, filter, and moisten the air, and can be worn under regular clothes (Mathieson, 2001). Similarly, a Romet filter looks like the neck of a lightweight sweater and is washable. It is also important for the person with a stoma to avoid getting water in it. Special stoma covers are available, to prevent water from entering the trachea during showering and bathing.

In addition to changing how the individual breathes, laryngectomy results in other physiological changes. The individual loses the ability to smell and, therefore, the ability to taste. Sometimes, a weakened sense of taste eventually returns.

Social, emotional, and psychological issues are likely to arise after surgery. Many laryngectomized people have difficulty adjusting to the change in their body image and suffer a loss of self-esteem. It can be very difficult to face the world with an obvious disfigurement such as a hole in the neck and wasted neck muscles following the neck dissection.

The major issue after surgery, especially after total laryngectomy, is the recovery of the ability to communicate. Even after partial surgery or radiotherapy, the individual's voice is likely to be dysphonic, and voice therapy is necessary and valuable. However, with total laryngectomy normal voicing is impossible, and the aim of treatment is to provide some way for the person to produce a functional voice. An alternative source of voicing must be generated, a process known as voice restoration.

Before the process of voice restoration is begun, it is advisable for the individual to meet with the speech–language pathologist, preferably before the surgery, and definitely immediately after the surgery. Many surgeons will schedule the patient to see a speech–language pathologist preoperatively, as they find this to be a valuable experience for the individual. At this session, the patient and his or her family can talk with the therapist regarding the surgical procedure, the rehabilitation process, different methods of voice restoration, likely problems postoperatively, and problems related to communication. During this visit, the clinician can assess the patient's communication abilities, as a way of preparing for postoperative communication. The more prepared the individual, the more likely he or she will respond positively to the surgery and to the voice restoration process. Sometimes during the preoperative visit, the therapist may bring along a laryngectomized speaker to help the patient understand that life after the surgery can be productive and happy. Even if such a meeting does not occur during the preoperative session with the patient, a meeting with a well-adjusted and communicative laryngectomized speaker is crucial during the postoperative session. Also during these early sessions, the clinician begins to introduce various options for communication. The speech–language pathologist may bring along different types of artificial larynges for the patient to try, if the surgeon finds that there is no medical reason to prevent this. Being able to communicate with an artificial larynx while still in the hospital can be very motivating for the patient.

Methods of Voice Restoration

There are three main methods of voice restoration: artificial larynx, esophageal speech, and tracheoesophageal speech. The individual may use one or a combination of methods, depending on his or her anatomical features, communication needs, motivation, cognitive functioning, hearing status, and preference.

Artificial Larynx

The artificial larynx is probably the quickest and easiest method of voice generation. Artificial larynges generate an external sound that can be transferred to the speaker's vocal tract and articulated into speech sounds. There are two primary ways of achieving this: pneumatic devices and electronic-type devices. Pneumatic devices are designed to take advantage of the individual's own pulmonary air. The device consists of a tube within which is a reed or membrane that vibrates in response to air passing over it (Slavin, 1997). At one end of the tube is a mouthpiece, and at the other is a stoma cover. The person inhales through the stoma, and then covers the stoma during exhalation, so that the air is forced through the tube, into his or her mouth. The sound that is generated is articulated into speech. The advantage of this type of system is that the speech, although low in pitch, is normal in terms of phrasing and does not sound robotic. However, this device requires two hands, one to cover the stoma and the other to hold the mouthpiece in place, making it inconvenient for everyday functioning.

Electronic-type devices do not depend on the speaker's respiratory system, but rather generate a tone electronically. In a manner similar to the pneumatic type, the tone is transmitted to the vocal tract, either via the neck or the mouth. The neck-type (transcervical) electronic instruments are the most popular. The individual holds the device firmly against his or her neck, and the sound is transmitted through the neck into the vocal tract. Speakers learn to use the on–off switch to coincide with voiced and voiceless sounds. Many different devices are available from numerous manufacturers, with different pitch- and volume-changing capabilities, as well as different weights, sizes, and shapes. The tone produced does tend to sound mechanical and robotic; however, some devices, particularly more current models, include switches and buttons to regulate pitch and intensity. These devices can be fairly sophisticated. For example, the Romet Speech Aid Electronic Larynx is equipped with both volume and pitch controls. The NuVois II Electronic Larynx Speech Aid has digital pitch and volume controls. The NuVois III and the Servox Digital Artificial Larynx are both digital devices.

Neck devices are suitable for individuals who have neck tissue on at least one side that is healthy, soft, and supple, to facilitate the transmission of the sound (Deem & Miller, 2000; Slavin, 1997). Also, the person must be able to use the various switches and to coordinate the sound with the beginning and ending of each utterance. It is more convenient if the individual can learn to use his or her nondominant hand to operate the device, leaving the dominant hand free for everyday use.

The mouth or intraoral device channels the electronically generated tone into a small plastic tube that the person holds in the mouth. The generator is contained in a small case, which the speaker can clip to an article of clothing or keep in a pocket. As with the neck-type device, the individual uses the on–off switch to coordinate appropriate voicing and articulation. The mouth-type device is often used immediately after surgery as it does not interfere with healing of the neck and throat area.

An important advantage of an artificial larynx is that it is easy to use and may be used very soon, or even immediately, after the surgery. Loss of voice is a frightening and disheartening experience, so the sooner the individual is able to communicate, the less psychological stress he or she will likely suffer. In addition, the speaker's intelligibility is typically good with an artificial larynx, even during the beginning of the learning process. Other advantages include the high intensity level, which can be very useful in noisy situations, and the low level of maintenance required. Some laryngectomees use an artificial larynx as their only means of voicing, whereas others use one while they are learning another method of voice production or as an adjunct for difficult speaking situations or when they are fatigued.

There are also some disadvantages, however, the chief one being the robotic and mechanical sound of the voice. In addition, use of the device is not totally convenient, as the speaker needs one hand to operate it. Overall, however, the artificial larynx is a valuable means of voice production for many laryngectomized individuals.

Esophageal Speech

Esophageal speech (ES) has traditionally been the most accepted form of alaryngeal speech, at least in the opinion of speech–language pathologists. Esophageal speech refers to speech that is produced by taking air into the esophagus and then releasing it through the pharynx. As the air is released, it vibrates the ring of muscle that controls the opening to the esophagus. This anatomical area, known as the pharyngo-esophageal (P-E) sphincter or segment, is made up of muscle fibers from the cricopharyngeus and inferior pharyngeal constrictor muscles. The resulting sound, while typically much lower pitched than normal voice, can become reasonably intelligible and acceptable. However, it is a difficult form of voicing to learn, and only around 33%–50% of laryngectomees are able to master this method (Slavin, 1997).

The major problem in achieving this form of voicing is that the individual has to learn to control the P-E segment opening. Ordinarily, the muscles comprising the P-E segment are contracted so that the segment is closed, to prevent air from being taken into the esophagus. Only during a swallow does the P-E segment relax, allowing the esophagus to open for the passage of food. It is not easy to train the esophagus to open voluntarily for the intake of air, and all methods of training for ES focus on teaching the individual to gain voluntary control of the P-E segment opening. When this goal is achieved, the individual's upper esophagus functions as an air reservoir, generating the necessary air supply for vibration of the P-E segment. The P-E segment, in effect, functions as the vibrating element that generates the voice signal. Sometimes, this new configuration is called the neoglottis ("new glottis").

The P-E segment differs from individual to individual in terms of its size, shape, length, mass, and location (Slavin, 1997), so there is wide variability in the resulting voice across individuals. In general, though, the neoglottis differs from the normal vocal folds in important ways. For example, while the normal vocal folds are able to vibrate at many different frequencies and amplitudes, and are able to finely regulate pitch and loudness, the neoglottis is a more massive structure, with considerably less fine motor control. Thus, the sound that is produced typically is much lower pitched for both males and females, often around one octave lower than a normal male voice. In addition, amplitude tends to be reduced by an average of 10 dB (Slavin, 1997). It is also much harder for the individual to vary pitch, so often the voice sounds monotonous. Rate of speech also differs from that of normal speakers. The normal rate is approximately 150–190 words per minute, while the average rate for esophageal speakers has been found to be around 85–130 words per minute. Several factors account for the slower rate. One is that esophageal speakers need to pause more often to replenish their air supply, because the esophagus holds far less air than the lungs. The typical esophageal speaker can produce only around 3–5 words per air intake, whereas normal speakers average around 12 words per breath.

Techniques of air intake include consonant injection, glossal press, and inhalation. The goal of these methods is to create a difference in air pressure either above or below the P-E segment, in order to briefly open the sphincter so that air can flow into the esophagus (called insufflation) and be released into the vocal tract. These methods may be facilitated because the normal pressure of the P-E sphincter is often reduced following laryngectomy. The aim of each method is to teach the speaker to insufflate and release the air as quickly as possible. To achieve proficient esophageal speech, the person should be able to produce 4–9 syllables per insufflation, with a speaking rate of 85–129 words per minute and good intelligibility.

The consonant injection method takes advantage of the fact that stops and fricatives are produced by building up and then releasing oral pressure. The oral pressure achieved may be great enough to overcome the resistance of the closed P-E segment. The individual is taught to time the oral pressure build-up of these consonants with the resulting insufflation, first in isolated sounds and syllables, and then eventually during connected speech.

The glossal press method uses the tongue like a piston to increase the oral air pressure above that of the P-E segment, so that the P-E segment will open and allow air to enter the esophagus. The dorsum of the tongue is pressed against the alveolar ridge or anterior portion of the hard palate in order to prevent air from escaping through the oral cavity. At the same time, the speaker pumps the rest of the tongue upward and backward to compress the air in the oral cavity, thereby increasing its pressure. It is important for the individual to keep the velopharyngeal passageway closed, to prevent air from exiting through the nasal cavities. This technique works well for phonemes that do not rely on high intraoral pressure.

In the inhalation method, rather than building up pressure in the oral cavity, the goal is to reduce pressure below the neoglottis. Inhaling through the stoma can substantially decrease the pressure within the esophagus, forcing the P-E segment to open and air to enter the esophagus.

Individuals may find one of these three techniques easier than the others, but for maximum benefit, the person should attempt to learn all three methods and use them as appropriate in connected speech. One thing that is of major importance is that the speaker should avoid swallowing the air, because the motoric patterns associated with swallowing are completely different from those associated with fluent esophageal speech (Duguay, 1991). In addition, swallowing air can result in a bloated and uncomfortable feeling. Duguay (1991) noted that esophageal speech needs to both sound good and look good. This means that the speaker needs to eliminate lip-smacking, head and shoulder movements, or any other distracting facial or bodily gestures that he or she might use to try to facilitate air intake. The person needs to learn good articulatory patterns to maximize intelligibility, and must learn to avoid stoma blasts and air klunking. Stoma blasts occur when the speaker pushes pulmonary air through the stoma with excess force. The individual must learn to expel the air more slowly to overcome this noisy exhalation, which can interfere with the intelligibility of speech. Air klunking can occur as the person insufflates the esophagus and probably results from too much air being used too quickly and with too much effort (Duguay, 1991).

As mentioned earlier, a rather small percentage of laryngectomized individuals learn to use esophageal speech proficiently. One reason that prevents more people from using ES is the occurrence of pharyngoesophageal spasm. This spasm occurs when muscles of the pharynx and esophagus constrict tightly, preventing the P-E sphincter from opening. Even when an individual does learn to produce esophageal voice, he or she may be unable to manipulate duration, intensity, pitch, quality, articulation, and prosody (Duguay, 1991). However, many laryngectomized individuals do learn to control these aspects of speech (Gandour & Weinberg, 1983; McHenry, Reich, & Minifie, 1982). The development of proficient esophageal speech can also be hindered by physical problems, such as hyper- or hypotonicity of the P-E sphincter, paralysis or weakness of the lip and/or tongue muscles, and hearing loss (Duguay, 1991). Persons with gastrointestinal problems may not be able to achieve esophageal speech, because the esophagus may not be able to hold the air charge (Slavin, 1997). Finally, psychological factors can play a role. It has been shown that individuals who live and interact with other people may achieve better esophageal speech than those who live alone (Shanks, 1995).

Tracheoesophageal Puncture

During the 1980s, Marc Singer, an otolaryngologist, and Eric Blom, a speech–language pathologist, developed a technique to channel air from a laryngectomized person's lungs directly from the trachea to the esophagus, thus bypassing the need to inject air from the oral cavity into the esophagus. This form of alaryngeal voice is considerably easier to produce than regular esophageal speech. Singer and Blom's notion was not new; indeed, many surgeons over some decades had tried to fashion some kind of shunt from the trachea to the esophagus, without success. What Singer and Blom did was to make a fistula (small hole) in the soft tissue wall that separates the trachea from the esophagus, and to insert a silicone prosthesis into this aperture. This prosthesis is a one-way valve that allows air from the trachea to enter the esophagus, while preventing food and liquid in the esophagus from escaping into the trachea. When the speaker closes the stoma, either manually with a finger or with a valve that fits into the stoma, exhaled air is directed through the prosthesis into the esophagus. Then, just as with esophageal speech, the air exits via the P-E sphincter, setting up vibration and voicing that is articulated in the normal way. A rubber catheter is inserted into the fistula for a period of time after the surgery, in order to keep the fistula open. For individuals who receive the tracheoesophageal puncture (TEP) at the same time as the laryngectomy, this hole can serve the double purpose of being used instead of a nasogastric tube for feeding.

The TEP method of voicing has great advantages over the traditional esophageal techniques. First, because the speaker does not have to learn a difficult new way of injecting air into the esophagus, this technique is more accessible to many more people. Second, because pulmonary air is used, a much larger supply of air is available for speech, whereas the esophageal supply is severely limited. The increased air supply allows a much greater degree of fluency, as the individual does not have to pause every few seconds to inject more air. Both rate of speech and phrasing, therefore, are much closer to normal; however, pitch still tends to be lower than normal, particularly for women, and intonation patterns are limited.

Another advantage of TEP speech is that the procedure can be done at the time of the laryngectomy or endoscopically at any subsequent time. Also, proficient TEP speech is often achieved within a very short time following the procedure, whereas it can take months or even years for a person to achieve esophageal speech.

It is important that candidates for the TEP procedure be selected carefully. To successfully use this method of speech, individuals need to be motivated, be mentally stable, have adequate manual dexterity and visual acuity to care for the stoma and the prosthesis, not have hypertonicity of the P-E segment, have adequate lung function, and have a stoma that is of the correct size to fit the prosthesis without compromising the airway. In addition, candidates should not be alcohol or drug dependent (Slavin, 1997). Candidates should also be free of systemic diseases, such as diabetes, that impair the healing of tissues (Slavin, 1997). If the individual has had radiation therapy, the TEP should not be performed until 6–12 weeks after the radiation, to allow healing to occur. Typically, an individual who chooses this procedure will have an esophageal insufflation test to determine whether the P-E segment is able to be vibrated by outgoing air. In this procedure a catheter is inserted through the nose and pharynx, and into the top of the esophagus. A valve is placed in the stoma, so that when air is blown into the catheter, it can be channeled through the esophagus rather than out the stoma. Air is then blown into the catheter, and as the air escapes through the P-E sphincter, it is noted whether or not the sphincter goes into spasm or shows any tightening. As the air escapes, the person is instructed to phonate various sounds, words, and phrases. If the sphincter does tighten or spasm, or if the individual is unable to sustain phonation for at least 8 seconds (Blom, Singer, & Hamaker, 1985), he or she may need a myotomy in order to produce voicing more easily. A myotomy is a procedure in which specific muscles in the P-E region are cut to prevent the muscular spasms. Another type of procedure to reduce muscle spasm is the pharyngeal plexus neurectomy in which the nerves that supply the pharyngeal constrictor muscles are sectioned (Deem & Miller, 2000). Recently, Botox injections have been used to temporarily paralyze or weaken the muscles, thus allowing for easier insufflation.

The prostheses used for TEP come in different lengths and sizes so they can be tailored specifically to the individual's physical characteristics. The best prosthesis will allow air to flow easily into the esophagus without completely blocking the stoma (Slavin, 1997). Once the best fit has been found, the speaker is taught to insert and remove the prosthesis for cleaning. Valves are available to regulate the flow of air through the stoma. The valve is sensitive to various degrees of pressure. It remains open for normal or heavy breathing, but it closes when the individual uses the pressures required for speech, thus diverting air through the prosthesis and out the esophagus. Over the past few years, a new type of prosthesis has become available for individuals with poor eyesight or limited manual dexterity, allowing them to become candidates for the TEP procedure. This indwelling, semipermanent prosthesis can remain in place for a period of several months to a year. The prosthesis can be cleaned while in place by the patient or caregiver, and should be changed after the appropriate interval of time by a speech–language pathologist or otolaryngologist (Lombard, 2006).

Summary

In general, although all three forms of alaryngeal speech—artificial larynx, esophageal, and tracheoesophageal—tend to be viewed by listeners as abnormal (mostly because of the low pitch), any of these methods of alaryngeal speech can be effective in promoting functional communication for laryngectomized individuals. Which one (or combination) the speaker chooses depends on his or her physical characteristics, communication needs, mental and emotional status, and other internal and external environmental factors.

Chapter 7
Clinical Management

Clinical management strategies for voice disorders can be broadly divided into two categories: medico-surgical and behavioral voice therapy (Ferrand, 1997). Medico-surgical treatments consist of drug therapy and/or surgical procedures. Behavioral voice therapy focuses on vocal education, vocal hygiene, and strategies for altering aspects of voice production. These two types of treatments are complementary to each other. For instance, after clients have polyps surgically removed from their vocal folds, they need to be taught a less abusive way of using the vocal mechanism to prevent the recurrence of the problem. Similarly, children whose vocal folds are scarred from frequent removals of papillomas must be encouraged to make the most efficient use of the vocal mechanism. The type of clinical management strategy that is chosen depends on the cause or causes and the symptoms of the disorder, as well as the individual's motivation, vocal needs, and lifestyle.

Phonosurgery

Phonosurgery is the name given to a group of different surgical procedures that have as their aim the preservation or restoration of the speaker's best possible voice (Ferrand, 1997). Phonosurgery differs from traditional concepts of laryngeal surgery, in which removal of the disease is the primary concern and the voice is of secondary importance. Phonosurgery procedures are those designed to shift the vocal folds into a better position for phonation; those used to alter the position or tension of the arytenoid cartilages and thus influence the vocal folds; some forms of cancer surgery, such as tracheoesophageal puncture; and different forms of thyroplasty and injection techniques such as Botox (Case, 2002). This chapter includes descriptions of the following phonosurgical procedures that can be performed for different vocal problems: laryngeal framework manipulation, arytenoid adduction, arytenoidectomy, laryngeal reinnervation, laser microsurgery, vocal fold injection, and Botox injection. Table 7.1 summarizes these procedures and their purposes.

Laryngeal Framework Techniques

Laryngeal framework surgeries have become popular in the treatment of vocal fold paralysis, bowing of the folds, and pitch disorders. These techniques involve changing the position and tension of the vocal folds by manipulating the surrounding cartilages. One type of laryngeal framework surgery, called thyroplasty, involves manipulation of the vocal folds through a window cut into the thyroid cartilage. Four types of thyroplasties have been classified based on the positioning of the vocal folds:

- Type I: Medialization
- Type II: Lateralization
- Type III: Relaxation
- Type IV: Stretching or lengthening

Type I, medialization, is the most commonly performed type of thyroplasty, typically in the case of unilateral vocal fold paralysis. The surgery is usually done with only a local anesthetic so that the person can phonate during the procedure. The thyroid cartilage is exposed, and a window is cut into it. The surgeon shapes a small wedge of a flexible synthetic material called Silastic. This wedge is inserted through the cartilage window and positioned behind the affected vocal fold, thus pushing the fold closer to the midline. During this portion of the procedure, the individual is asked to phonate. Different voice qualities are obtained by

TABLE 7.1 PHONOSURGICAL PROCEDURES AND THEIR PURPOSES

Procedure	Purpose
Laryngeal framework techniques	To change the position and tension of the vocal folds by manipulating the surrounding cartilages
Arytenoid adduction techniques	To rotate vocal processes medially, with the goal of approximating the posterior portion of the vocal folds
Arytenoidectomy	To remove an arytenoid cartilage so as to widen the glottis
Laryngeal reinnervation	To take a pedicle of muscle with an intact nerve supply, or a nerve itself, from another area of the body and attach it to the affected laryngeal muscle
Laser microsurgery	To perform a precise, delicate removal of lesions and diseased tissue
Vocal fold injection	To increase the bulk of a paralyzed vocal fold to bring it closer to midline
Botox injection	To weaken hyperfunctional muscles to reduce laryngo-spasms

manipulating the degree of medialization and glottal closure, and the speech–language pathologist and speaker can decide on the optimal voice quality. The Silastic implant is then sutured in place, and the larynx is closed (Blaugrund, Isshiki, & Taira, 1992).

There are several benefits to this procedure. First, the Silastic insert can be adjusted at any time after the surgery to increase or decrease the degree of medialization. Second, the medial edges of the vocal folds are unaffected, so that vibration can occur along a smooth edge. Third, the person is awake during part of the procedure, so he or she plays an active role in determining optimal voice quality. Fourth, chances of an allergic or immune response to a foreign substance within the vocal folds (as can occur with Teflon injection) are reduced. However, it is important that the implant be positioned very accurately, because if it is too high or too low, the paralyzed vocal fold will be vertically out of alignment with the intact fold, resulting in a poorer voice quality. Usually, the speech–language pathologist monitors both the position of the vocal folds and the resulting voice quality, using nasoendoscopy and auditory-perceptual techniques.

Type I thyroplasty is also used in problems other than paralysis. For example, medialization may be effective in improving voice and swallowing function in elderly patients with vocal fold bowing (Linville, 2001; Postma, Blalock, & Koufman, 1998; Slavit, 1999).

The other types of thyroplasties are not as common, although Type IV is used in situations where a higher pitch is desired, such as transgender voice treatment. Thyroplasty Type IV (cricothyroid approximation) involves moving and suturing the thyroid and cricoid cartilages toward each other in order to achieve the elongation and tensing of the vocal folds that normally occur for a higher pitch. One variant of the procedure involves increasing vocal fold tension by placing a suture around the inferior horn of the thyroid and passing it under the cricoid anteriorly, pulling it taut (Zeitels, Hillman, Desloge, & Bunting, 1999).

Arytenoid Adduction

Sometimes medialization by itself is not enough to produce an optimal voice quality for a speaker with unilateral vocal fold paralysis. If the paralyzed fold is shorter than the intact fold, or if the affected arytenoid cartilage is rotated outward, then effective vocal fold closure cannot be achieved, even with medialization (Linville, 2001). Arytenoid adduction involves rotating the vocal process medially, thus allowing a closer approximation of the posterior portion of the vocal folds. The vocal process is sutured in position to provide permanent improvement in closure. However, it is important for the surgeon to avoid overrotation of the affected vocal process, which can result in less than optimal vocal fold position and negatively affect voice quality.

A variant of this type of procedure is adduction arytenopexy (Zeitels, Hochman, & Hillman, 1998). This technique avoids the possibility of overrotation by positioning the arytenoid on the medial aspect of the cricoid articular facet in a way that is closer to its normal adduction during phonation. Thus, the normal synergistic action of the vocal fold adductors and abductor muscles is facilitated. Zeitels et al. (1998) reported that, compared to the classic procedure, the adduction arytenopexy procedure resulted in greater lengthening of the vocal fold, higher vocal fold positioning, and a more normally contoured arytenoid.

Arytenoidectomy

A different type of procedure is necessary in situations requiring increased vocal fold abduction rather than increased adduction. The most common procedure is arytenoidectomy, which involves removing an arytenoid cartilage. The person is anesthetized, and a CO_2 laser is used to remove the entire arytenoid cartilage along with the posterior end of the thyroarytenoid muscle. The posterior portion of the vocal fold is sutured in an appropriate position. This kind of procedure is done to widen the glottis, usually in cases where the individual has airway obstruction and dyspnea. Removing an arytenoid cartilage widens the posterior glottis. Widening the posterior glottis is very effective in improving the adequacy of the airway, because the posterior glottis accounts for approximately 60% of the entire glottal area (Colton, Casper, & Leonard, 2006). Also, the anterior glottis is not widened as much, helping to preserve the speaker's best possible voice.

Laryngeal Reinnervation Techniques

In some cases of unilateral vocal fold paralysis, the surgeon attempts to restore nerve function to the affected muscles, a process called reinnervation. With medialization techniques, even when the affected fold is brought closer to the midline, it can still atrophy and become increasingly flaccid. Laryngeal innervation techniques can be beneficial in preventing atrophy of the affected fold. In this type of procedure, a pedicle of muscle with an intact nerve supply, or a nerve itself, is taken from another area of the body and attached to the affected laryngeal muscle. The nerve supply to the healthy transplanted pedicle is transferred to the paralyzed muscle, providing an alternate source of innervation. In this procedure it is important to select a donor muscle that is compatible with the paralyzed laryngeal muscle. The strap muscles of the neck are often used as donors, because the neck muscles are involved in breathing, which may facilitate firing of the affected muscle (Case, 2002). This type of procedure in conjunction with other medialization techniques may meet most of the short- and long-term needs of patients with unilateral paralysis (Tucker, 1999).

Laser Microsurgery

The development of laser technology has benefited laryngeal surgery immensely by reducing bleeding, swelling, and scarring during and after surgery. The laser is used in conjunction with an operating microscope, which allows detailed inspection of laryngeal structures, as well as very precise and delicate removal of lesions and diseased tissue.

Vocal Fold Injection

Injecting a paralyzed vocal fold with some kind of suitable substance has been a popular method of treating unilateral vocal fold paralysis for many decades. The injected substance provides increased bulk to the affected fold, thus making it easier for the healthy fold to cross over the midline and achieve increased contact with the paralyzed fold. Stronger medial compression is thereby achieved, resulting in a stronger and less breathy voice quality. The substance is injected either via the mouth (transoral) or through the skin (transcutaneous). Transoral injections may be done using a laryngeal mirror or a direct laryngoscope. Transcutaneous injections are inserted through the cricothyroid membrane. The procedure is done under local anesthetic, with specially designed needles.

The most commonly used substance is Teflon paste, which is injected deep within the vocalis muscle, lateral to the arytenoid cartilage (Kieff & Zeitels, 1996). However, there are some disadvantages with Teflon. First, the substance may migrate to other locations, leaving the vocal fold with an irregular contour that interferes with vibration. Second, some individuals have an allergic response to Teflon, which can result in the formation of granulation tissue around the substance, a condition sometimes called Teflon granuloma. Third, the exact placement of the paste is critical. Injection that is too medial or too superior can impair the vibration (Stemple, Glaze, & Klaben, 2000). Fourth, the procedure is not reversible, because the substance infiltrates into the surrounding tissues (Kieff & Zeitels, 1996). Because of these disadvantages, many voice centers no longer use Teflon.

Other substances such as collagen and autologous fat are also used for injection. Collagen is similar in its cellular structure to vocal fold tissue, which increases its compatibility to the host tissue and decreases the risk of an allergic response and granulation formation. Another advantage of collagen is that it tends to soften existing scar tissue, and thus enhances vocal fold vibration (Linville, 2001; Stemple et al., 2000). A bovine form of collagen used to be employed, but currently autologous collagen injections are being developed (*autologous* refers to a substance that occurs normally in a certain type of tissue or structure). Also, autologous fat is sometimes used. This substance is soft and flexible, and minimizes the chances of an allergic response. However, the fat is reabsorbed by the vocal fold tissues, so reinjection is necessary every 2–3 months (Case, 2002).

Botox Injection

For individuals with spasmodic dysphonia, Botox is injected. Botox is the medical form of a toxin related to botulism. As a disease, botulism is often fatal because it is a toxin that paralyzes muscles. However, when used medically, the toxin reduces muscle spasms and has been used extensively and successfully to treat focal dystonias such as blepharospasm, oromandibular dystonia, and spasmodic torticollis (Case, 2002). Botox prevents the transmission or release of acetylcholine at the myoneural junction, essentially creating a flaccid paralysis. The procedure involves injection of the Botox into the vocalis muscle for adductor spasmodic dysphonia (SD) and into the posterior cricoarytenoid muscle in the case of abductor SD. The needle is passed through the cricothyroid membrane, which has been locally anesthetized. Electromyography is used to monitor the muscle activity and to make sure that the needle has been properly placed.

For the first week or two after the injection, the speaker's voice may be weak and breathy, and he or she may have some slight difficulty in swallowing. Thereafter, the voice stabilizes, and the individual is able to talk with much less effort and strain. The positive effects last 2–4 months, and then the person's voice starts to revert to the preinjection level. Most people are reinjected every few months. Many clinicians have reported that behavioral voice therapy in conjunction with Botox lengthens the time between injections. For the adductor form of spasmodic dysphonia, the Botox is usually injected through the cricothyroid membrane into the vocalis muscle, under local anesthetic. For the abductor version, the drug is injected into the posterior cricoarytenoid muscle.

Behavioral Voice Techniques

Behavioral voice techniques can be used to address symptoms of the voice problem, including hoarseness, breathiness, tension, and inappropriate pitch; physiological function such as hypo- or hyperadduction; or the cause of the problem, such as vocal abuse. The following discussion focuses on vocal hygiene programs; techniques to minimize hyperfunctional and hypofunctional voice use; and techniques for some specific voice disorders, including paradoxical vocal fold disorder, chronic cough, transgender voice, and hypokinetic dysphonia resulting from Parkinson's disease.

Vocal Hygiene

Vocal hygiene programs focus on eliminating or reducing vocally abusive behaviors and promoting less hyperfunctional phonatory patterns. Typically, these programs include some or all of the following components (see Table 7.2).

- *Vocal education.* Most individuals have only a vague awareness of their larynx and do not realize that the larynx is a delicate and complex organ, subject to stresses and injuries. The more knowledgeable the client, the more likely it is that he or she will be motivated to comply with a therapy program.

TABLE 7.2   TYPICAL VOCAL HYGIENE PROGRAM

Vocal education

Identification of vocal abuses

Compensatory vocal behaviors

Hydration

Easy onset techniques

Identification of other causes

- *Identification of vocal abuses.* Although some clients may recognize their vocally abusive behaviors, many individuals may not be aware of the damaging effects of hyperfunction and abuse. It may be helpful to construct a chart listing the person's daily activities and the amount and type of voice used for each. Smoking and alcohol use should be included as abusive behaviors.
- *Facilitation of compensatory behaviors.* The clinician and client are partners in devising strategies to reduce vocal abuse that are consistent with the individual's lifestyle. Expecting a person to completely alter his or her lifestyle or profession is not usually a realistic goal. For example, a teacher with nodules is more likely to agree to wear a small wireless microphone during class than to find a different job with fewer vocal demands.
- *Vocal fold lubrication.* It is important to keep the vocal folds well hydrated. Research has shown that it is more difficult to set the vocal folds into vibration when they are dehydrated. In turn, dehydration can result in greater vocal effort and resulting vocal fatigue. Many clinicians recommend that clients drink a minimum of 48–64 ounces of water per day. Clients should also be encouraged to avoid beverages with caffeine. Increasing water intake and reducing caffeine intake help to maintain hydration of the whole body, including fluid secreted by the glands in the laryngeal ventricle that keep the vocal folds moist.
- *Easy onset of phonation.* There are several techniques that are designed to promote a less abusive onset of phonation, such as using the yawn–sigh technique to ease into phonation; using a slightly breathy voice during conversation; and using a "confidential" voice (see descriptions of these techniques below).

Techniques such as these may be extremely helpful in improving the quality of the voice.

- *Identification of other factors that may be contributing to the vocal problem.* As mentioned previously, factors such as allergies, gastroesophageal reflux disease (GERD), medications, and stress, may cause or may coexist with the voice problem. These factors need to be addressed in addition to the vocal abuse, and it may be necessary to refer the client to an appropriate professional such as an allergist, endocrinologist, or gastroenterologist.

Techniques for Hyper- and Hypofunctional Voice Use

Hyperfunction is typically addressed by helping the individual to reduce the force of vocal fold closure during vibration. Commonly used techniques include easy onset of voice to prevent hard glottal attacks at voice initiation; phonating with a slightly breathy quality; the yawn–sigh technique to relax the intrinsic and extrinsic laryngeal musculature; and massage and manipulation of the external larynx to reduce tension (Ferrand, 1997). Table 7.3 lists the techniques used to improve hyperfunctional voice use, and the techniques are described below.

Techniques to address hypofunctional voice include those aimed at increasing the force of vocal fold closure by either strengthening muscles normally used for phonation or activating accessory muscle groups that are generally not involved in voice production, or a combination of both (Karnell, 1991). Methods include isometric exercises such as pushing down strongly on a chair while simultaneously phonating; using a hard glottal attack to initiate phonation; or using coughing and throat clearing (which both use high levels of muscular energy) as preparatory strategies to initiate phonation (see Table 7.3).

TABLE 7.3   TECHNIQUES TO REDUCE HYPER- AND HYPOFUNCTIONAL VOICE USE

Yawn–sigh	Yawn and then gently sigh, while focusing on the relaxed sensation in the throat area.
Breathy voice	Use a slightly breathy voice, which reduces the force of vocal fold closure during vibration.
Confidential voice	Speak with a voice that is low in intensity and slightly breathy, which reduces the overall level of intrinsic and extrinsic laryngeal muscle tension.
Resonant voice	While speaking, feel vibrations around the nose and mouth area, and lightly approximate vocal folds to facilitate improved projection with less effort.
Vocal function exercises	Increase bulk, strength, and coordination of laryngeal and respiratory musculature by vocal warm-ups, pitch glides, and maximum vowel prolongation at selected pitches.
Laryngeal manipulation	Decrease intrinsic and extrinsic laryngeal muscle tension.
Pushing	Push down strongly on a chair while simultaneously phonating

Yawn–Sigh

The yawn–sigh technique is designed to help the client develop a more relaxed and open throat posture while phonating. The individual is instructed to yawn and then gently sigh, focusing on the relaxed sensation in his or her throat area while doing so. Once the client is accustomed to the relaxed posture, phonation is introduced in place of the sigh, and the yawn is faded gradually to a normal breath.

Breathy Voice

Using a slightly breathy voice can reduce the force of vocal fold closure during vibration, as the flow of air between the vocal folds prevents them from making excessive contact. The client can be instructed to use this type of voice for specified periods during the day to reduce the load on the laryngeal mechanism. It is emphasized to the client that breathy voice is different from a whispered voice.

Confidential Voice

Confidential voice is produced at a low intensity and is slightly breathy, but is not a whisper. The reduction in intensity reduces the excessive contact between the vocal folds and reduces the overall level of intrinsic and extrinsic muscle tension (Branski, Murry, & Rosen, 2005). This strategy is typically recommended for clients who are recovering from vocal fold injury or phonosurgery. Typically, this type of voicing pattern is used for 2–3 weeks while the vocal folds heal.

Resonant Voice

In resonant voice, which is easy to produce, the vocal vibrations are felt in the "mask" of the face, that is, around the nose and mouth area. The client is taught to produce sound in a more "forward" position, with the focus away from the laryngeal area. Humming nasal sounds (/m/, /n/) and saying words beginning with nasals (e.g., "me," "knee") is a strategy used to achieve this goal, and the individual may find it helpful to place his or her fingers on the mask area to feel the vibrations. During this type of phonation, the vocal folds should just barely approximate, reducing the effort required to phonate. Abdominal breathing may also be useful in focusing effort away from the laryngeal area and providing a more effective power source for speech. This type of speech has been shown to project well without being overly forceful (Smith, Finnegan, & Karnell, 2005).

Vocal Function Exercises

Exercising the vocal folds is based on similar principles to exercising other body structures. Systematic exercise is designed to increase bulk, strength, and coordination of laryngeal and respiratory musculature (Branski et al., 2005; Verdolini, 1998). Steps include vocal warm-up, pitch glides (high to low and low to high), and maximum prolongation of /o/ at selected pitches. Each exercise is completed twice, and the entire program is done twice a day. It is important for the client to use a resonant voice without strain while doing the exercises.

Accent Method

The accent method is used more in Europe than in the United States. This method involves coordinating abdominal breathing with a relaxed open throat sensation while phonating. To promote this kind of easy, coordinated phonation, the client is trained to use rhythmic whole-body movements simultaneously with phonation. The individual vocalizes rhythmic consonant sounds (called accents) in time with body movements and abdominal breath support for each accent. As the client progresses, utterances become increasingly complex and eventually are carried over to the conversational level. The whole-body movements are faded over time.

Laryngeal Manipulation

The laryngeal manipulation technique may be useful in cases of muscle tension dysphonia. In most cases of vocal hyperfunction, the larynx is in an elevated position due to excessive muscular tension. Individuals often report neck pain associated with the tension. The goal of manipulating the laryngeal area is to decrease the muscle tension. The clinician focuses on specific laryngeal areas by placing the thumb and forefinger in the thyrohyoid space and massaging in small circles, starting at the front portion of the thyroid cartilage and moving toward the back. As the clinician does the massage, he or she can also exert slight downward pressure on the larynx, and gently move the larynx from side to side. The massage generally begins at a superficial level, with the depth increasing depending on the degree of tension and the person's tolerance for the procedure (Ford & Bless, 1996). During the massage the client vocalizes a sustained vowel or hums, and the clinician points out any improvements in voice quality. The individual is also asked to note any reductions in pain and tenderness. Once the laryngeal and supralaryngeal musculature are more relaxed and an improved voice quality is obtained, the clinician and client work to lengthen the utterances while maintaining the muscular and vocal improvement. This technique has been shown to be effective in reducing tension and improving voice quality in many cases (e.g., Van Lierde, De Ley, Clement, De Bodt, & Van Cauwenberge, 2004).

Pushing

The pushing technique can be used in cases of weak, breathy voice resulting from hypofunction. The technique is based on the notion that combining phonation with some kind of large effortful body motion helps to increase the force of vocal fold vibration. The client is instructed to push down hard on a flat surface such as a chair or table while vocalizing. This facilitates a stronger voice, and the pushing is gradually reduced as the individual learns to produce the higher effort voice in more complex utterances and in everyday situations. A similar technique is to pull up hard on a surface rather than pushing down. It is important to keep in mind that the pushing and pulling strategies are based on creating a hyperfunctional manner of vocal fold vibration, and should be used with caution in order to avoid damage to the laryngeal mechanism.

Behavioral Therapy Techniques for Specific Disorders

Paradoxical Vocal Fold Disorder

Behavioral voice therapy has been found to be very helpful for many people with paradoxical vocal fold disorder (PVFD). Because speech–language pathologists are trained in laryngeal anatomy and physiology, they are well equipped to teach the client how to control his or her laryngeal function for respiration. These clinicians help clients to learn a more effective breathing pattern, such as using more abdominal musculature and focusing the effort away from the laryngeal area. Manual circumlaryngeal muscle tension techniques (see "Laryngeal Manipulation" previously described) may also be beneficial in helping the person to relax the laryngeal area.

A program for an individual with PVFD focuses on providing emotional support, teaching more effective ways of breathing, helping him or her to keep a relaxed and open throat, exploring and developing strategies to deal with emotional stressors, and identifying and managing triggers that precipitate attacks. A critical objective of therapy is to generalize the new breathing patterns and strategies to everyday life.

So-called respiratory retraining programs have been described for PVFD as well as for chronic cough. As suggested by Sandage (2006) and Murry, Tabaee, and Aviv (2004), an important first step in such a program is training the individual to become aware of subtle changes in his or her body that might signal the onset of an attack. The individual is taught to use progressive relaxation techniques to develop an awareness of tension around both the laryngeal and the neck and face areas. Once this awareness is developed, the person learns how to consciously relax the muscles and to use this strategy to relax the entire body during an attack (Cookman, n.d.). The next step is to train the person to use a more efficient abdominal breathing pattern. Once the client is adept at this, he or she learns to breathe in a rhythmic manner, with a shorter breath in and a longer breath out, and then to time the exhalation with phonation. As the individual becomes more adept at this easy rhythmic breathing, he or she is taught to breathe out with more resistance, by producing voiceless fricative sounds such as /sh/ or /s/. This helps the person to avoid sudden inspiratory bursts that interrupt the normal breathing pattern (Murry et al., 2004). The third step involves training the client to use specific breathing patterns (the "breathing recovery") to keep the vocal folds open when feeling the onset of an attack. One such method involves sniffing in deeply through the nose using the abdominal muscles. This helps to open the vocal folds very quickly. After the sniff, the individual exhales as fully as possible on a voiceless fricative for 8–10 seconds, which helps to maintain the vocal folds in an abducted position.

Other strategies that can be taught for relaxed breathing and speaking include laryngeal massage, resonant voice, and easy onset (see previous descriptions). The sufferer should be encouraged to become aware of any early warning symptoms, so he or she can put strategies into effect before the onset of an attack.

Chronic Cough

Behavioral treatment for chronic cough is based on identifying triggers for the cough and finding ways to reduce or eliminate it. The client should seek medical treatment to determine if allergies, postnasal drip, or GERD is contributing to the cough. The individual should also be encouraged to reduce or eliminate other agents or practices that may be contributing to or worsening the cough, including menthol cough drops, gargling, a dry environment, mouth breathing, and foods that can cause reflux (Sandage, 2006), such as caffeine, chocolate, spicy foods, and so on.

Charting the coughing behavior on a daily basis for a week or two and noting any precipitating factors (specific aromas, fumes, foods, etc.) can help the client to bring the behavior to conscious awareness. Once triggers are identified, the individual can learn to substitute other behaviors in the presence of the triggers, such as sucking on ice chips, drinking cold water, or using a hard swallow in place of the cough. Other behaviors that may be used when the person feels an impending cough include blowing slowly through pursed lips, whistling, and humming (Gallena, 2007). A program of respiratory retraining as described above for PVFD may also be useful for chronic cough.

Transgender Voice

Although raising pitch is an important focus for feminizing the sound of the male-to-female transgender voice, addressing other aspects of communication may be equally or more effective. Techniques that have been suggested as effective in raising pitch include practicing a soprano "head voice" while avoiding falsetto; use of the yawn–sigh technique to prevent vocal strain and hyperadduction; and circumlaryngeal manipulation to reduce laryngeal tension. Practice in using more feminine intonational patterns and inflections and in using more feminine language structures (e.g., adding tag questions after a statement) is also critical. Habituating a confidential voice (described previously) may create a slightly breathy voice quality, which also could enhance the perception of femaleness. Individuals should also learn to emphasize and stress words using pitch increases, which is a feminine characteristic, rather than using volume increases, which is a masculine characteristic.

Other markers of gender voice identity include pitch range and variability. Female speakers typically use a wider range of fundamental frequencies (F0s) and a more varied pattern of pitch inflections, whereas male speakers tend to use a more restricted F0 range and fewer intonational patterns (Ferrand & Bloom, 1996). Women's intonational patterns differ from men's not only in range but also in phrase endings. Women tend to use more rising inflections at the ends of utterances, often giving their speech a somewhat tentative sound.

It is crucial to have the individual tape-record and critically evaluate the new vocal patterns at regular intervals during the therapeutic process. In addition, the use of feedback from instruments such as the Visi-Pitch or Computerized Speech Lab, both from Kay Elemetrics, is helpful in habituating and generalizing the newly learned strategies.

Attention should also be paid to articulation, vocabulary, and body language. Andrews (1995) suggested that, to sound more feminine, male-to-female transsexuals need to learn to speak more softly, use breathier onsets and a less forceful style, and use more smoothly linked phrasing patterns. Deem and Miller (2000) emphasized that these individuals should avoid certain vocal acts that are more commonly used by males, such as throat clearing, low-pitched vocalized pauses, and coughing. It is also important to avoid the use of falsetto, which has a thin reedy quality that does not sound natural or pleasant. Males wishing to be perceived as female sometimes use this register in the mistaken belief that the very high pitch will be helpful. In fact, a male who uses a lower pitch that is accompanied by a more feminine intonational pattern and style will sound more feminine than one who uses a higher pitch but fewer feminine patterns.

Adler et al. (2006) presented a systematic program for vocal therapy for the male-to-female transgender client. The program focuses initially on determining how the client perceives her own communication needs and what her expectations for therapy are. Situations are identified in which communication problems exist. Therapy then targets activities that help the client to increase her awareness of gender differences in both verbal and nonverbal areas. The client and clinician set goals based on the client's needs and expectations. The individual also learns about good vocal hygiene, as well as effective breath support through abdominal breathing. Relaxation exercises may be appropriate. Adler et al. noted that the specific types of therapeutic strategies that are implemented depend on the level of physiological and social support available to the individual. For example, for a client who has difficulty modifying pitch and who has few supportive social networks, Adler et al. suggested increasing the focus on counseling, as well as targeting vocal features other than pitch, such as intonation, resonance, rate and volume, articulation, language, and nonverbal behavior. A client who has a good support system needs less emphasis on counseling and therefore can concentrate more on various aspects of pitch control and other vocal issues.

Physical appearance is another important factor to take into account. Van Borsel, De Cuypere, and den Berghe (2001) and Adler et al. (2006) found that the perception of a male-to-female transsexual as male or female was affected by both physical appearance and vocal characteristics. They suggested that vocal training to feminize the voice should be done in conjunction with appearance factors such as clothing and makeup. An individual with a less feminine sounding voice may still be accepted as a woman if her physical appearance is convincingly female. One surgical technique that focuses on appearance is the laryngeal shave. This technique is designed to decrease the prominence of the Adam's apple by removing the upper portion of the anterior thyroid. The result is a more feminine looking neck.

Articulation should also be addressed, with the client being taught to articulate more gently yet with more precision than is typical of males. Nonverbal gender markers need work as well, such as maintaining eye contact, using touch and gestures more frequently, and so on. Thus, treatment is best provided in a holistic context, with emphasis not only on vocal characteristics but also on the person's overall communicative style and presentation.

Parkinson's Disease

Weak intensity is the hallmark of voice in Parkinson's disease. The behavioral treatment of choice for this problem is Lee Silverman Voice Treatment (Ramig, Countryman, Hoehn, O'Brien, & Thompson, 1996; Ramig, Countryman, Horii, & Thompson, 1995). The primary goal of this approach is for the speaker to increase loudness by using more forceful vocal fold adduction and to maintain the increased loudness by "recalibrating" the laryngeal mechanism.

For optimal results, this systematic approach to voice therapy is prescribed for 4 consecutive weeks at 4 sessions per week. Clients are trained to increase the force of vocal fold adduction and may use pushing or pulling techniques to help in this process. Individuals focus on high vocal effort, which overrides the rigidity and hypokinesia of the vocal folds (Herndon, 1997). This intensive treatment increases the likelihood that the client will gradually but systematically build up and maintain higher levels of vocal effort. It also helps the individual to understand and accept the increased amount of muscular effort needed to consistently increase vocal loudness to a higher level. Clients are also required to practice the new loudness level outside the clinic, to help them get used to using the increased effort level on a consistent basis. The end goal of the program is for the person to use the louder voice automatically in daily communication.

Appendix A
Laryngeal Structures and Functions

STRUCTURE	FUNCTION
Bone	
Hyoid bone	Is the point of suspension for larynx
Cartilages	
Thyroid	Attaches to vocal folds at anterior commissure
Cricoid	Is most inferior portion of larynx
Epiglottis	Protects larynx during swallowing
Arytenoids	Attach to vocal folds at vocal processes
Corniculates	Have no specific function
Cuneiforms	If present, may stiffen aryepiglottic folds
Joints	
Cricoarytenoids	Allow arytenoid cartilages to rock back and forth and glide medially and laterally, facilitating vocal fold abduction and adduction
Cricothyroids	Allow thyroid cartilage to tilt inferiorly and superiorly, facilitating pitch changes
Extrinsic membranes	
Hyothyroid	Connects hyoid bone to thyroid cartilage

Cricothyroid	Connects thyroid cartilage to cricoid cartilage
Cricotracheal	Connects cricoid cartilage to first tracheal cartilage

Valves

Aryepiglottic folds	Open during phonation; pull epiglottis downward and backward to close entrance to larynx during swallowing
False (ventricular) folds	Open during phonation; close for effortful laryngeal closure
True vocal folds	Close for phonation; open for breathing and voiceless sounds
Epithelium together with superficial lamina propria	Make up cover of vocal folds
Intermediate lamina propria together with deep lamina propria	Make up vocal ligament
Vocalis muscle	Makes up body of vocal folds

Extrinsic laryngeal muscles

Suprahyoids

Digastric	Elevates larynx during swallowing
Geniohyoid	Elevates larynx during swallowing
Mylohyoid	Elevates larynx during swallowing
Stylohyoid	Elevates larynx during swallowing

Infrahyoids

Omohyoid	Lowers larynx during swallowing
Sternohyoid	Lowers larynx during swallowing
Sternothyroid	Lowers larynx during swallowing
Thyrohyoid	Lowers larynx during swallowing

Intrinsic laryngeal muscles

Lateral cricoarytenoid	Adducts vocal folds
Interarytenoid	Adducts vocal folds
Posterior cricoarytenoid	Abducts vocal folds
Cricothyroid	Tenses vocal folds
Vocalis	Forms body of vocal folds

Appendix B
Terminology

Abduction.   Movement away from the midline.

Adduction.   Movement toward the midline.

Aphonia.   Complete absence of vocal fold vibration. An aphonic individual may be able to whisper.

Breathiness.   Audible leakage of air during vibration due to incomplete or inadequate vocal fold closure. The turbulent noise produced results in the breathy voice quality.

Diplophonia.   The perception of two pitches heard simultaneously.

Dysarthria.   Umbrella term for neurogenic disorders resulting in muscle weakness, paralysis, or lack of coordination of the speech subsystems (respiration, phonation, articulation).

Dysphonia.   Generic term for vocal dysfunction that results in disturbances in vocal quality, pitch, or loudness.

Dyspnea.   Subjective perception of difficulty in breathing.

Falsetto register.   Vocal register with a very high range of fundamental frequencies; also called *loft*.

Focal.   Limited to a specific area.

Functional disorder.   Dysphonia that has no evident anatomical or physiolological basis.

Fundamental frequency.   Rate of vibration of the vocal folds, measured in hertz. Correlates with the perception of pitch.

Glottal.   Relating to the vocal folds.

Harshness.   Vocal quality resulting from a combination of hoarseness and breathiness.

Hoarseness.   Refers to the perception of noise in the voice; also known as *roughness*.

Hyperfunction.   Voice produced with excessive muscular tension, often resulting in a pressed or strained quality.

Hypernasality.   Perception of excessive nasal resonance.

Hypofunction.   Voice produced with inadequate muscular tension, often resulting in a breathy and/or weak quality.

Hyponasality.   Perception of inadequate nasal resonance, particularly on nasal sounds.

Intensity.   Acoustic measure correlating with perceived loudness.

Jitter.   Acoustic measure of irregularity in the frequency of vocal fold vibration. Although all normal voices have a slight degree of jitter (less than 1%), higher levels can result in the perception of hoarseness or roughness.

Laryngitis.   Any inflammation of the larynx.

Loudness.   Volume of sound perceived by a listener. The acoustic correlates of loudness are amplitude and intensity.

Lumen.   Hollow space inside a tube, such as the larynx.

Lysis.   Surgical division of tissues that have adhered together, such as laryngeal webs.

Modal register.   Voice register that uses a middle range of fundamental frequencies. This is the register used most commonly in normal conversational speech.

Mucosal wave.   Undulating movement of the vocal folds during vibration, contributing to the rich and resonant sound of the human voice. Any interference with the mucosal wave results in some form of dysphonia.

Organic disorder.   Disorder caused by a specific structural or physiological defect.

Pedunculated.   Growth attached by a thin stalk to a base.

Phonation.   Creation of voiced sound by means of vocal fold vibration.

Phonosurgery.   Any type of surgery performed on the vocal folds to restore or improve vocal function with the least damage to the vocal fold tissues.

Pitch.   The perception of a tone as high or low on a musical scale, depending on its fundamental frequency.

Pitch break.   A sudden shift upward or downward in pitch.

Pressed voice.   Strained voice quality created by hyperfunctional vocal fold vibration and excessive subglottal pressures.

Psychogenic disorder.   Voice disorder caused by psychological factors. Such factors can result in structural changes to the larynx.

Pulse register.   Voice register that uses a very low range of fundamental frequencies. Also called *glottal fry*, *vocal fry*, or *creaky voice*.

Sessile.   Growth that has a broad base of attachment.

Shimmer.   Acoustic measure of irregularity in the amplitude of vocal fold vibration. Normal voices are characterized by a slight degree of shimmer (.5 dB or less).

Strain-strangle.   Voice quality characterized by extreme effort in production.

Stridor.   Noisy breathing that can occur on inspiration or expiration, typically due to airway obstruction.

Synechia.   Adhesion of tissues.

Tremor.   Regular vocal fluctuation in frequency, amplitude, or both. Tremors range from slow (4 Hz) to fast (15 Hz), depending on the underlying cause.

Vocal fatigue.   Perception of increased effort to produce voice.

Voice rest.   Client either is not allowed to speak at all for a specified amount of time or is temporarily restricted in voice usage.

Whisper.   Sound created by turbulent airflow exiting the partially closed vocal folds, rather than by vocal fold vibration.

Appendix C
Informative Websites

Chapter 2: Structural Disorders

Contact Granulomas
http://www.emedicine.com/ent/topic603.htm

Laryngomalacia
http://www.bcm.tmc.edu/oto/grand/21094.html

Recurrent Respiratory Papillomatosis
http://www.rrpf.org/rrpf/publications/TaskForceGuidelines
.htm

San Diego Center for Voice and Swallowing Disorders
http://www.sandiegovoice.org/stenosis%20and%20tracheoto
my.html

Subglottic Stenosis
http://www.utmb.edu/otoref/Grnds/Subgot-sten-9904/Subglot-
sten-9904.htm

Chapter 3: Inflammation and Irritation of the Larynx

Can't Breathe! Suspect Vocal Fold Dysfunction!
http://www.cantbreathesuspectvcd.com/page9.html

Department of Otolaryngology/Head and Neck Surgery at
Columbia University and New York Presbyterian Hospital
http://entcolumbia.org

Chapter 4: Nonorganic Disorders

Selected Mutism
http://www.asha.org/public/speech/disorders/Selective-Mutism
.htm

Chapter 5: Neurogenic Disorders

Amyotrophic Lateral Sclerosis
  http://www.alsa.org

Essential Tremor
  http://www.parkinsonsinstitute.org
  http://www.wfubmc.edu/surg-sci/ns/tremor.html

Huntington's Disease
  http://www.hda.org.uk/download/acrobat/hdafs002.pdf
  http://www.hdsa.org
  http://www.kumc.edu/hospital/huntingtons
  http://www.neurologychannel.com
  http://www.hda.org.uk/download/acrobat/hdafs009.pdf

Multiple Sclerosis
  http://www.neurologychannel.com/multiplesclerosis/symptoms
  .shtml
  http://www.nationalmssociety.org

Myasthenia Gravis
  http://www.myasthenia.org
  http://www.neurologychannel.com/myastheniagravis/treatment
  .shtml

References

Adler, R., Hirsch, S., Mordaunt, M., Hooper, C., Kozan, A., Van Borsel, J., et al. (2006, November). *Voice and communication therapy for the transgender client: Clinical guidelines.* Seminar presented at the American Speech-Language-Hearing Association annual convention, Miami.

American Joint Committee on Cancer. (2002). *Cancer staging manual* (6th ed.). New York: Springer-Verlag.

American Psychiatric Association. (2000). *Diagnostic and statistical manual of mental disorders* (4th ed., text rev.). Washington, DC: American Psychiatric Association.

American Speech-Language-Hearing Association Special Interest Divisions, Voice and Voice Disorders. (2002–2006). *Consensus auditory–perceptual evaluation of voice.* Rockville, MD: Author.

Andersson, K., & Schalen, L. (1998). Etiology and treatment of psychogenic voice disorder: Results of a follow-up study of thirty patients. *Journal of Voice, 12,* 96–106.

Andrews, M. L. (1995). *Manual of voice treatment: Pediatrics through geriatrics.* San Diego, CA: Singular.

Andrianopoulos, M. V., Gallivan, G. J., & Gallivan, K. H. (2000). PVCM, PVCD, EPL, and irritable larynx syndrome: What are we talking about and how do we treat it? *Journal of Voice, 14,* 607–618.

Angsuwarangsee, T., & Morrison, M. (2002). Extrinsic laryngeal muscular tension in patients with voice disorders. *Journal of Voice, 16,* 333–343.

Aronson, A. E., & DeSanto, L. W. (1983). Adductor spastic dysphonia: Three years after recurrent laryngeal nerve resection. *Laryngoscope, 93,* 1–8.

Atoynatan, T. H. (1986). Elective mutism: Involvement of the mother in the treatment of the child. *Child Psychiatry and Human Development, 1,* 15–27.

Awan, S. N. (2001). *The voice diagnostic protocol: A practical guide to the diagnosis of voice disorders.* Gaithersburg, MD: Aspen.

Baker, J. (2002). Psychogenic voice disorder—Heroes or hysterics? A brief overview with questions and discussion. *Logopedics, Phoniatrics, Vocology, 27,* 84–91.

Baltaxe, C. A. M. (1994, November). *Communication issues in selective mutism.* Paper presented at the American Speech-Language-Hearing Association Convention, New Orleans.

Bertino, G., Bellomo, A., Ferrero, F. E., & Ferlito, A. (2001). Acoustic analysis of voice quality with or without false vocal fold displacement after cordectomy. *Journal of Voice, 15,* 131–140.

Blager, F. (2000). Paradoxical vocal fold movement: Diagnosis and management. *Current Opinion in Otolaryngology Head and Neck Surgery, 8,* 180–183.

Blalock, P. D. (1992). Breath support. *The Visible Voice, 1,* 6–7.

Blaugrund, S. M., Isshiki, N., & Taira, T. (1992). Phonosurgery. In A. Blitzer, M. E. Brin, C. T. Sasaki, S. Fahn, & K. S. Harris (Eds.), *Neurologic disorders of the larynx.* New York: Thieme Medical.

Blitzer, A., Lovelace, R. E., Brin, M. F., Fahn, S., & Fink, M. E. (1985). Electromyographic findings in focal laryngeal dystonia (spasmodic dysphonia). *Annals of Otology, Rhinology, and Laryngology, 94,* 591–594.

Blom, E. D., Singer, M. L., & Hamaker, R. C. (1985). An improved esophageal insufflation test. *Archives of Otolaryngology, 111,* 211–212.

Bloom, R. L., & Ferrand, C. T. (1997). Neuromotor speech disorders. In C. T. Ferrand & R. L. Bloom (Eds.), *Introduction to organic and neurogenic disorders of communication: Current scope of practice* (pp. 166–192). Boston: Allyn & Bacon.

Boone, D. R., McFarlane, S. C., & Von Berg, S. L. (2005). *The voice and voice therapy* (7th ed.). Boston: Pearson Allyn & Bacon.

Branski, R. C., Murry, R., & Rosen, C. A. (2005). *Voice therapy.* Retrieved June 9, 2007, from http://www.emedicine.com/ent/topic683.htm

Buckmire, R. A. (2001). *Arytenoid fixation.* Retrieved June 9, 2007, from http://www.emedicine.com/ent/topic609.htm

Caputo Rosen, D., & Sataloff, R. T. (1998). Psychological aspects of voice disorders. In R. T. Sataloff (Ed.), *Vocal health and pedagogy* (pp. 243–255). San Diego, CA: Singular.

Case, J. L. (2002). *Clinical management of voice disorders* (4th ed.). Austin, TX: PRO-ED.

Chronic cough. (n.d.). Voice & Swallowing Center, College of Physicians and Surgeons, Columbia University at New York Presbyterian Hospital. Retrieved June 10, 2007, from http://www.voiceandswallowing.com/Voicedisorders_cough.htm

Colton, R., Casper, J. K., & Leonard, D. (2006). *Understanding voice problems: A physiological perspective for diagnosis and treatment* (3rd ed.). Baltimore: Lippincott Williams & Wilkins.

Cookman, S. M. (n.d.). *Paradoxical vocal cord dysfunction.* Retrieved June 9, 2007, from http://72.14.205.104/search?q=cache:aT6ZS3Vb22YJ:www2.uchc.edu/otomain

Darley, F. L., Aronson, A. E., & Brown, J. R. (1969). Differential diagnostic patterns of dysarthria. *Journal of Speech and Hearing Research, 12,* 246–256.

De Biase, N., Master, S., Pontes, P., & De Biase, S. (2001). Laryngeal posterior granulomas: Follow-up after Botox injection. *Brazilian Journal of Otorhinolaryngology, 67,* 557.

Deem, J. F., & Miller, L. (2000). *Manual of voice therapy* (2nd ed.). Austin, TX: PRO-ED.

Doyle, P. C. (1997). Voice refinement following conservation surgery for cancer of the larynx: A conceptual framework for treatment intervention. *American Journal of Speech–Language Pathology, 6,* 27–35.

Duguay, M. J. (1991). Esophageal speech training: The initial phase. In S. J. Salmon & K. H. Mount (Eds.), *Alaryngeal speech rehabilitation* (pp. 47–78). Austin, TX: PRO-ED.

Edan, G., & Coustans, M. (2000). Is immunosuppression a future therapeutic strategy for multiple sclerosis? *Pathology and Biology (Paris), 48,* 114–120.

Eicher, S. A. (1991). *Recurrent respiratory papillomatosis.* Retrieved June 9, 2007, from http://www.bcm.tmc.edu/oto/grand/111691.html

Farrell, A., Theodoros, D., Ward, E., Hall, B., & Silburn, P. (2005). Effects of neurosurgical management of Parkinson's disease on speech characteristics and oromotor function. *Journal of Speech, Language, and Hearing Research, 48,* 5–20.

Feldman, M., Nixon, J. V., Finitzo-Hieber, T., & Freeman, F. J. (1984). Abnormal parasympathetic vagal function in patients with spasmodic dysphonia. *Annals of Internal Medicine, 100,* 491–495.

Ferrand, C. T. (1997). Structurally related and neurogenic voice disorders. In C. T. Ferrand & R. L. Bloom (Eds.), *Introduction to organic and neurogenic disorders of communication: Current scope of practice* (pp. 247–272). Needham Heights, MA: Allyn & Bacon.

Ferrand, C. T. (2007). *Speech science: An integrated approach to theory and clinical practice* (2nd ed.). Boston: Allyn & Bacon.

Ferrand, C. T., & Bloom, R. L. (1996). Gender differences in children's intonational patterns. *Journal of Voice, 10,* 284–291.

Finitzo, T., & Freeman, F. (1989). Spasmodic dysphonia; whether and where: Results of seven years of research. *Journal of Speech and Hearing Research, 32,* 541–555.

Ford, C. N., & Bless, D. M. (1996). *Muscle tension dysphonia and spasmodic dysphonia: The role of manual laryngeal tension reduction in diagnosis and management.* Paper presented at the American Laryngological Association, Orlando, FL.

Fakaura, H., Kent, S. C., Pietrusewicz, M. J., Khoury, S. J., Weiner, H. L., & Hafler, D. A. (1996). Induction of circulating myelin basic protein and proteolipid protein-specific Transforming Growth Factor-beta Z-secreting Ths T cells by oral administration of myelin in multiple sclerosis patients. *Journal of Clinical Investigation, 98,* 70–77.

Gallena, S. K. (2007). *Voice and laryngeal disorders: A problem-based clinical guide with voice samples.* St. Louis, MO: Mosby Elsevier.

Gandour, J., & Weinberg, B. (1983). Perception of intonational contrasts in alaryngeal speech. *Journal of Speech and Hearing Research, 26,* 142–148.

Garnett, J. D. (2005a). *Contact granulomas.* Retrieved June 10, 2007, from http://www.emedicine.com/ent/topic603.htm

Garnett, J. D. (2005b). *Subglottic stenosis in adults.* Retrieved from http://www.emedicine.com/ent/topic 499.htm

Gelfer, M. P., & Schofield, K. J. (2000). Comparison of acoustic and perceptual measures of voice in male-to-female transsexuals perceived as female versus those perceived as male. *Journal of Voice, 14,* 22–33.

Giannoni, C. M. (1994). *Laryngomalacia*. Retrieved June 10, 2007, from http://www.bcm.tmc.edu/oto/grand/21094.html

Giddan, J. J., Ross, G. J., Sechler, L. L., & Becker, B. R. (1997). Selective mutism in elementary school: Multidisciplinary interventions. *Language, Speech, and Hearing Services in Schools. 28*, 127–133.

Gold, L. (1999). Voice training for the transsexual. *VASTA Newsletter, 13*, 10. Retrieved June 10, 2007, from http://www.vasta.org/newsletter/99/summer03.html

Gray, R. F., & Rutka, J. A. (1988). *Recent advances in otolaryngology*. London: Longman Group.

Gross, M. (1999). Pitch-raising surgery in male-to-female transsexuals. *Journal of Voice, 13*, 246–250.

Harman, E. M. (2002). *Recurrent respiratory papillomatosis*. Retrieved June 10, 2007, from http://www.emedicine.com/med/topic2535.htm

Henkel, J. (1998). Parkinson's disease: New treatments slow onslaught of symptoms. *FDA Consumer, 32*. Retrieved June 10, 2007, from http://www.fda.gov/fdac/features/1998/498_pd.html

Herndon, G. (1997). *The Lee Silverman Voice Treatment*. Retrieved June 10, 2007, from http://mick.murraystate.edu/cdi624/fall97/slvrman.htm

Hoehn, M. H., & Yahr, M. D. (1967). Parkinsonism: Onset, progression and mortality. *Neurology, 17*, 427–442.

Holmes, R. L., & Fadden, C. T. (2004, May 1). Evaluation of the patient with chronic cough. *American Family Physician, 69*. Available from http://www.aafp.org/afp/20040501/2159.html

Jacobson, B. J., Johnson, A., Grywalski, C., Silbergleit, A., Jacobson, G., Benninger, M. S., et al. (1997). The Voice Handicap Index (VHI): Development and validation. *American Journal of Speech–Language Pathology, 6*, 66–70.

Johnson, A. F. (1994). Clinical voice assessment. In M. S. Benninger, B. H. Jacobson, & A. F. Johnson (Eds.), *Vocal arts medicine: The care and prevention of professional voice disorders*. New York: Thieme Medical.

Johnson, N. (2001). Tobacco use and oral cancer: A global perspective. *Journal of Dental Education, 65*, 328–339.

Karnell, M. P. (1991). Adjunctive measures for optimal phonosurgical results: The role of voice therapy. In C. N. Ford & D. M. Bless (Eds.), *Phonosurgery: Assessment and surgical management of voice disorders* (pp. 213–224). New York: Raven Press.

Kent, R. D. (1994). *Reference manual for communicative sciences and disorders: Speech and language.* Austin, TX: PRO-ED.

Kieff, D., & Zeitels, S. (1996). Phonosurgery. *Comprehensive Therapy, 22,* 222–230.

Koschkee, D. L., & Rammage, L. (1997). *Voice care in the medical setting.* San Diego, CA: Singular.

Koufman, J. A. (1996). Infectious and inflammatory diseases of the larynx. In J. J. Ballenger & J. B. Snow (Eds.), *Otorhinolaryngology* (15th ed., pp. 535–555). Philadelphia: Williams & Wilkins.

Koufman, J. A., & Blalock, P. D. (1988). Vocal fatigue and dysphonia in the professional voice user: Bogart-Bacall syndrome. *Laryngoscope, 98,* 493–498.

Lee, J. (2001). Management of congenital laryngeal web. *The Bobby R. Alford Department of Otorhinolaryngology and Communication Sciences Grand Rounds Archives.* file://C:/DOCUME-1/Carole/LOCALS-1/Temp/triFPOAB.htm

Leeper, H. A., Parsa, V., Jamieson, D. G., & Heeneman, H. (2002). Acoustical aspects of vocal function following radiotherapy for early T1a laryngeal cancer. *Journal of Voice, 16,* 289–302.

Lin, C.-L.-G., Bristol, L. A., Jin, L., Dykes-Hoberg, M., Crawford, T., Clawson, L., et al. (1998). Aberrant RNA processing in a neurodegenerative disease: The cause for absent EAAT2, a glutamate transporter, in amyotrophic lateral sclerosis. *Neuron, 20,* 589–602.

Linville, S. E. (2001). *Vocal aging.* San Diego, CA: Singular/Thomson Learning.

Lombard, L. (2006). Laryngectomy rehabilitation. *eMedicine.* Retrieved July 27, 2007, from http://www.emedicine.com/ent/topic312.htm

Mathers-Schmidt, B. A. (2001). Paradoxical vocal fold motion: A tutorial on a complex disorders and the speech pathologist's role. *American Journal of Speech–Language Pathology, 10,* 111–125.

Mathieson, L. (2001). *Greene and Mathieson's the voice and its disorders* (6th ed.). Philadelphia: Whurr.

McClay, J. E. (2006). *Recurrent respiratory papillomatosis*. Retrieved June 10, 2007, from http://www.emedicine.com/ent/topic594.htm

McHenry, M., Reich, A., & Minifie, F. (1982). Acoustic characteristics of intended syllabic stress in excellent esophageal speakers. *Journal of Speech and Hearing Research, 25,* 554–564.

Merati, A. L., Heman-Ackah, Y. D., Abaza, M., Altman, K. W., Sulica, L., & Belamowicz, S. (2005). Common movement disorders affecting the larynx: A report from the Neurolaryngology Committee of the AAO-HNS. *Otolaryngology–Head and Neck Surgery, 133,* 654–665.

Moorhead, J. C. (2006). *Cysts of the larynx*. Retrieved June 10, 2007, from http://www.bcm.tmc.edu/oto/grand/91491.html

Morris, M. J. (2006). Vocal cord dysfunction and asthma. *Business Briefing: US Respiratory Care,* pp. 1–5.

Morrison, M., Rammage, L., & Emami, A. J. (1999). The irritable larynx syndrome. *Journal of Voice, 13,* 447–455.

Murry, T., Tabaee, A., & Aviv, J. E. (2004). Respiratory retraining of refractory cough and laryngopharyngeal reflux in patients with paradoxical vocal fold movement disorder. *The Laryngoscope, 114,* 1341–1345.

Newman, D., & Ramadan, N. (1998). Neurologic disorders: An orientation and overview. In A. Johnson & B. Jacobson (Eds.), *Medical speech–language pathology: A practitioner's guide* (pp. 211–242). New York: Thieme Medical.

Newman, K. B., Mason, U. G., & Schmaling, K. B. (1995). Clinical features of vocal cord dysfunction. *American Journal of Respiratory and Critical Care Medicine, 152,* 1382–1386.

Orlikoff, R. F., & Kraus, D. H. (1996). Dysphonia following nonsurgical management of advanced laryngeal carcinoma. *American Journal of Speech Language Pathology, 5,* 47–52.

Pontes, P., Kyrillos, L., Behlau, M., De Biase, N., & Pontes, A. (2002). Vocal nodules and laryngeal morphology. *Journal of Voice, 16,* 408–414.

Postma, G., Blalock, P., & Koufman, J. (1998). Bilateral medialization laryngoplasty. *Laryngoscope, 108,* 1429–1434.

Powell, D. M., Karanfilov, B. I., Beechler, K. B., Treole, K., Trudeau, M. D., & Forrest, L. A. (2000). Paradoxical vocal cord dysfunction in juveniles. *Archives of Otolaryngology–Head and Neck Surgery, 126,* 29–34.

Ramig, L., Countryman, S., Hoehn, M., O'Brien, C., & Thompson, L. (1996). Intensive speech treatment for patients with Parkinson's disease: Short and long term comparison of two techniques. *Neurology, 47,* 1496–1504.

Ramig, L., Countryman, S., Horii, Y., & Thompson, L. (1995). A comparison of two forms of intensive speech treatment for Parkinson's disease. *Journal of Speech and Hearing Research, 38,* 1232–1251.

Rammage, L., Morrison, M., & Nichol, H. (2001). *Management of the voice and its disorders* (2nd ed.). Vancouver, BC: Singular/Thomson Learning.

Rosen, C. A., & Murry, T. (2000). Voice Handicap Index in singers. *Journal of Voice, 14,* 370–377.

Rosen, C. A., & Soose, R. J. (2006). *Vocal fold paralysis, unilateral.* Retrieved June 10, 2007, from http://www.emedicine.com/ent/topic347.htm

Rosenfield, D. (1991). Pharmacologic approaches to speech motor disorders. In D. Vogel & M. Cannito (Eds.), *Treating disordered speech motor control.* Austin, TX: PRO-ED.

Roy, N., Ford, C. N., & Bless, D. M. (1996). Muscle tension dysphonia and spasmodic dysphonia: The role of manual laryngeal tension reduction in diagnosis and treatment. *Annals of Otology, Rhinology, and Laryngology, 105,* 851–856.

Sandage, M. (2006, July 11). Sniffs, gasps, and coughs: Irritable larynx syndrome across the lifespan. *The ASHA Leader, 11*(9), 16–17, 20.

Santer, D. M., & D'Alessandro, M. P. (n.d.). *Virtual hospital: Electric airway: Upper airway problems in children: Subglottic stenosis.* Retrieved 2002 from http://www.vh.org/Providers/Textbooks/ElectricAirway/Text/SubStenosis.html

Sataloff, R. T., Castell, D. O., Katz, P. O., & Sataloff, D. M. (2006). *Reflux laryngitis and related disorders* (3rd ed.). San Diego, CA: Plural.

Schweinfurth, J., & Ossoff, R. (2001). *Sulcus vocalis.* Retrieved June 10, 2007, from http://www.emedicine.com/ent/topic605.htm